Winning at
BUSINESS
NEGOTIATIONS

Winning at BUSINESS NEGOTIATIONS

A GUIDE TO PROFITABLE DEAL MAKING

COLIN ROBINSON

KOGAN
PAGE

KPMG Peat Marwick Management Consultants

First published in 1990 by
Kogan Page Ltd,
120 Pentonville Rd, London N1 9JN

Typeset by J&L Composition Ltd, Filey, North Yorkshire
Printed and bound in Great Britain by Richard Clay Ltd,
Bungay, Suffolk

British Library Cataloguing in Publication Data

A CIP catalogue record for this book is available from the British
Library.

ISBN 0–7494–0224–5

CONTENTS

The purpose of commercial negotiation is to create an economic benefit to the negotiator that would not otherwise have been obtained

Aims of this book

'... the simple plan,
that they should take who have the power,
and they should keep who can.'

William Wordsworth
Rob Roy's Grave

ORIGINS

I had always wanted to write a book.

I was never sure whether it would be a thriller, a travel book or a major academic text. As it has turned out, it is none of these. I hope, however, that it is a valuable contribution to the many people who, inadvertently or by intent, become involved in commercial negotiation. There is, after all, no reason why they should not enjoy the activity.

Sometime during 1985, it was becoming increasingly clear to me that many of the people that I met from both industry and commerce felt that they had a lot to learn about negotiation. They were sure they could be achieving far better and tighter deals than they were.

To help fill a gap, I launched a series of intensive one-day training sessions in negotiating skills, initially aiming these at the buyer rather than the vendor. These seminars proved popular and successful and are still being run, albeit in different form, as I have learned a great deal from the students while teaching these skills.

This led to a number of advisory assignments with clients who must unfortunately remain unnamed. During this time, it became very clear that many people were involved over and over again in negotiations but remained uncertain about how to approach them. Some, indeed, were quite frightened, because they were never sure what was expected of them as negotiators.

Quite by chance, I was then asked to fill a vacant speaking spot at short notice. The audience was a group of academic heads of department at a course being run by Surrey University. The only topic on which I had notes readily available was negotiation. We talked about the art of selling university research effort to the private sector and concentrated on negotiation aspects. The planned 90 minute session ran for about four hours, but the discussion was lively and constructive. I learned a lot: I hope the audience did. They remained awake, which might say more about the staying power of academics than the content of the lecture and discussion!

On returning the following year to give the same session (necessarily a little shorter!), a fortunate meeting with Professor John Adair prompted the suggestion that the various lectures and advisory engagements that I had undertaken in commercial negotiating were good material for a book.

There are already many books which deal with negotiation. Why write another?

The specific objectives of this book are dealt with below. Suffice it to say that, even with the number of books available, most people do not feel that they are well served by them. Many are not obtaining the best deals, many never negotiate and many others know that they negotiate badly. If this is the case, the other books are not doing the job that they presumably set out to do.

In this book, a lot of effort has gone into relating negotiating skills to everyday business situations. The style adopted is to identify approaches, attitudes, techniques and tricks that have meaning to the circumstances that we might meet every day, with the aim of ensuring that negotiation becomes an everyday tool for everyone involved in commercial activity of any kind. As with other tools, if you cannot enjoy negotiating, you will try to avoid it; then, if you cannot avoid negotiating, you will do it badly.

But there is also another aim. Other books address only those who are actually negotiating and not those who have the responsibility of managing negotiators and of monitoring and controlling their work. The use of many personal anecdotes from authors

'. . . and now let me tell you how I brilliantly concluded yet another negotiation . . .'

may make interesting light reading and some can be most valuable. Such stories should not be the only significant content.

Here, then, the aim is to instruct, help, advise and support. It is the intention that readers in more senior management roles be put into the position where they can ask questions such as:

- What strategy do you have?

- What skills will you employ?

- What are the review points?

- What are your expectations from each stage?

- What is the balance of effort and return?

- How will you monitor your own success?

- How will *I* know if you have succeeded?

and be able to discuss answers constructively.

CONTENT

Most books that have been written on the subject of negotiation, together with the majority of lectures and published articles, try to cover every aspect of the topic. They therefore include:

- Summit meetings between national leaders.

- Annual wage negotiations with trades unions.

- Attempts to release hostages.

- International trade negotiations, for example GATT.

Hidden somewhere deep in the text, but certainly not highlighted for the general reader with a job to do, will be *day to day buying, selling and resolving problems*.

An all-embracing approach misses the point that, in many situations, the political and emotional factors in negotiation far outweigh the commercial influences. Negotiation can easily become primarily a matter of personal achievement. In commercial negotiations political, emotional and personal involvement must be (and can be) minimized. In other types of negotiation, any one of these factors may well become a major influence.

This highlights an interesting feature about negotiators. There are those who say that negotiation is a single skill which can be applied in every circumstance. This is a dangerous and simplistic view. For example, much as we might admire the Robert Maxwells, Lord Kings and Professor Roland Smiths of this world for their determination and ability to achieve their targets in negotiation, how many of us would want such people negotiating to save our lives if we were held hostage?

This book concentrates on commercial negotiations, generally where there are willing buyers and sellers, but equally where barter deals are being sought. It assumes that there is intended to be a positive business outcome from the negotiations – not that litigation is a possibility from the start. In effect, it looks at negotiations where both parties have a direct financial interest in the satisfactory outcome of the discussions.

The question of litigation is an important one to clarify from the outset. Negotiation should *never* be started with the view that it must end in the courts. If the position is that agreement *cannot* be reached by the negotiators, then one is not strictly negotiating but is setting up a position ready to influence others who will subsequently sit in judgement. There are certainly aspects of negotiation techniques that are appropriate in these circumstances, but such conditions are by no means those of free negotiation.

We are, therefore, considering deals entered into willingly by the parties concerned, involving both goods and services and covering both the private and public sectors. Much of the content of the book applies equally well to deals which we do in our private lives as to our business activities.

The carpet sale

A   Well, a very fine carpet if I may say so, Madam. A very discerning choice. I would have that one myself if only I could afford it. Still, it is a pleasure to be privileged to sell it to someone who appreciates fine things.

B   I see what you mean. But it is extremely expensive. In fact, far too expensive.

A   Well, not for what you would be getting. .... Ah, it does not show the discount for prompt orders on that ticket, does it?

B   No.

A   Well, if you order today and I can get the paperwork into this evening's post, I can offer you an 8 per cent discount on the marked price. And, of course, we will be facing a supplier's price increase on Wednesday that will have to be passed on to the customer.

B   I will leave it then. It is already over my budget and I would not like to order it until my sister sees it – she's very good on interior design and I appreciate her opinion. She could not get in here before Thursday. Thank you anyway for your attention.

A   Well, our manager is on holiday at the moment and, if I could be sure it was Thursday and could move quickly on the paperwork, and if it was for more than 20 square metres. ...

The essence of negotiation is that it is not about winning or losing – it is about striking a deal which is satisfactory to both sides. Of course, your efforts should be directed towards ensuring that it is more satisfactory to your side than to the other.

If one of the negotiators holds all the aces and the other knows it, then we are not talking about true negotiation but simply about squeezing out as much gain for the person with all the advantages, regardless of the wishes or needs of the other.

Thus, in a true commercial negotiation, both parties have something to offer and something to gain

The strategic element

Two factors which often seem to be lacking in works on commercial negotiation, and in many of the seminars and longer training courses on the subject, are:

- The place of negotiation in the overall buying or selling process.
- The planning of the whole negotiation, rather than simply the selection of a few techniques.

These shortcomings arise because it is much more enjoyable to write and read about the techniques and tactics of negotiating than about developing the underlying strategies.

A significant part of this book is given over to the planning and preparation that should take place before a negotiation even starts. This looks at what the negotiator is trying to achieve in both the short and longer terms and at how the single negotiation fits in with the wider business picture. In that respect, the book attempts to redress the balance between strategy and tactics and to present a more balanced picture than is usual.

How much really is negotiable?

A favourite saying of the hawks in negotiating is that:

Everything is negotiable

They infer that you should challenge everything that your opponent puts up and take some advantage of every single one of the issues involved. This can be a dangerous approach for the great majority of situations in which commercially oriented people find themselves.

There is certainly merit in looking at all of the features arising in a deal and assessing which may be open to challenge, but the biggest problem in attacking everything lies in the fact that it diverts your attention away from those issues which are most important to you. If you gain some ground on a point almost irrelevant to you, perhaps your opponent will be seeking some form of concession in return on an issue which you do feel to be important.

You may certainly choose to debate issues that are not critical to you simply to obscure those which are important. You may also choose to probe a wide range of the issues involved to identify your opponent's flexibility. However, the over-aggressive 'everything is negotiable' approach, generally accompanied by the need to snatch concessions of any size on every issue, is not constructive in the hands of the great majority of people and in the great majority of commercial circumstances.

In general, the most profitable strategy is to assess where you want to make gains from negotiation, rank and target gains in order of importance and then develop the tactics for achieving your objectives.

OBJECTIVES

This book aims to satisfy eight principal objectives.

Objective 1
To demonstrate that negotiation is not difficult.

Objective 2
To show that negotiation may be undertaken at many levels of sophistication.

Objective 3
To illustrate that all of us are negotiators already, even if we are not particularly good at it.

Objective 4
To highlight that negotiation can be fair, reasonable and ethical.

Objective 5
To put negotiation into perspective as a tool of strategic planning.

Objective 6
To assist negotiators find the most appropriate approach in any circumstances.

Objective 7
To make us all into better commercial negotiators.

Objective 8
To prove that commercial negotiation, while being productive, can also be enjoyable.

NEGOTIATION CAN BE LEARNED

Negotiation is without doubt a skill that can be learned – just like most other skills.

'But be not afraid of greatness; some men are born great, some achieve greatness, and some have greatness thrust upon them.'

William Shakespeare
Twelfth Night

It is quite appropriate to substitute negotiation for greatness in this famous quotation. Some people certainly are born with considerable talents as negotiators but, just like kings and queens born to greatness, they benefit from training and management development. Some people achieve greatness as negotiators through practice and from exposure to different and difficult circumstances, while yet others are thrown into negotiations at the deep end and have to do the best they can.

In whichever circumstances you find yourself, it is important to bear in mind that, however good or bad a negotiator at the moment, appropriate reading, training, practice and debate will enhance your skills and ensure that you are soon achieving worthwhile results and enjoying commercial negotiations.

The difficult daughter

A   Dad, can I have a lift into town tonight? We'd have to pick up Melissa and Jane but they'll both be ready. Leave about half past seven?

B   Well, yes, but can you give a hand with the washing up so that everything is cleared before we go out? I don't want your mother left with it all.

A   But Dad, I've homework to get done for tomorrow and I'll only just be able to finish it before I go out.

B   Well, you've been watching television for some time. If the work is so important, why haven't you been getting on with it?

A   Dad, I've got to have some leisure time. I can't work all the time. I do get on with my homework without being told to. You just want me to work all the time. I'm not a slave you know. I work better with a few breaks.

B   Well, all I'm asking is that you help out a bit around the house. I don't think that's unreasonable. Don't get so worked up about it.

A   Oh God. All right, I promise to help out tomorrow and the day after and the day after that and every day just as soon as my homework and revision are done. Is that what you want?

B   Well ... what time do you want to go out?

Moral 1
Some people are born negotiators. When you deal with them, know what you are taking on.

Moral 2
Do not enter into a negotiation unless you have a reasonable expectation of winning. Know your strengths and weaknesses. Do not grant concessions without gaining them. Ensure that you have a clear fallback position.

2

When and why to negotiate

KNOWING WITH WHOM TO NEGOTIATE

Colleagues

Let us consider first the occasions when one has to negotiate with colleagues at work. This might occur when one person has an objective to achieve and requires assistance or resources from another, who may not identify immediately any particular advantage in helping. Indeed, the achievement of one person's goals may even be perceived as detrimental to the interests of the other.

When in this position, one is generally not negotiating about money but about personal inconvenience, additional workload, tighter time-scales or increased risk of failure. It is necessary to demonstrate to one's counterpart that there is benefit in some form in giving assistance, either personally or to the corporate objectives. It may also be necessary to trade offers of help on each other's projects so that both can see advantage in the deal.

In negotiating with colleagues, the one who gains the most is the person who has prepared the arguments best, rehearsed counter arguments and thought through how to demonstrate benefits to the other person.

Probably the most common form of negotiation with colleagues arises when setting annual budgets and capital expenditure plans. Conventional wisdom is that each department puts in for at least twice what it thinks it will be awarded, hoping that the inevitable cutbacks will leave them enough to operate with in the following year.

Everyone knows how some departments always seem to be cut back less, to have more scope for spending and clearly to have the ear of the finance people. Of course, there are managers who manoeuvre themselves into this position by all manner of devices but generally they have observed the first rule of negotiation:

> **Prepare thoroughly**

They are able to go into their negotiations having been thoroughly briefed and with their arguments and counter arguments well thought through and researched.

Another very common instance of negotiating with colleagues arises between users of goods and services and the buyers responsible for obtaining them. Initially the user has to explain to the departmental head why the particular items are needed, why the full quantities requisitioned have to be obtained all at the same time and what will happen if they are not obtained soon.

Having moved satisfactorily through this negotiation, the user may then have to persuade the buyer why the items cannot be standard, why delivery cannot be delayed to help the organization's cash flow and why the delivery required is much sooner than the standard lead time. We will look in more detail at the buyer's role in this type of negotiation later in this chapter.

Salespeople

Mention negotiation to most people (except salespeople, of course) and they will think of buying things at work or at home. What is more, they will almost always think of price negotiation only. This is not particularly surprising. The great majority of sales negotiations are concerned only with the price of the goods or services in question. Later we will examine the other features that may be negotiated profitably.

In general, people selling things are better trained than people buying things. They are often, therefore, more aware of negotiating techniques and of the features of the deal that are open to negotiation. But they will not tell the buyer of the negotiable features unless pushed to do so. And why should they?

One of the objectives of this book is to make both buyers and sellers better negotiators so that they can more often reach mutually agreeable deals. The onus, then, is not upon the vendor to mention the negotiable features but for the buyer to find them.

Buyers

Buyers are often assumed to hold the position of greatest power in negotiating. However, they are generally not in the position of power that they often appear to be. For a start, they often do not have enough time to obtain the most appropriate contract terms because they have been given the specification of the user's requirements too late. Second, they will be subject to a variety of internal policies regarding sourcing, prices, cash flow, deliveries and so on. Third, unless they are very fortunate, they do not have enough time in their day to do all the research recommended in the best textbooks on buying and negotiating.

The buyer has a particular problem in negotiating that is worth highlighting here, as it applies to many other circumstances as well. In order to establish what is on the market that might satisfy a specified need, the buyer approaches a number of suppliers who have products that appear likely to do the job. As more and more suppliers' products are seen, the buyer's knowledge increases and the user may also change the specification on the basis of this increased information. Thus the increase in understanding is taking place during the very meetings when the buyer wishes to undertake preliminary negotiations with suppliers.

Although this cannot be avoided entirely, the successful buyer makes best use of the time available by receiving effective technical briefing and knowing as much as possible about the commercial terms operating in the market concerned. In other words, it comes back to the basic rule of negotiation that one should do one's preparation and background work thoroughly before being exposed to the opposition.

In negotiating with buyers in your own organization, it is worth bearing in mind the difficulties and constraints which they face. *Never put someone who is on your own team into the position of being unable to negotiate effectively with the opposition.*

• *NOT NEGOTIATING AT ALL* •

An electricity distribution company with an extensive network of overhead and underground cables was approached by a private company that wanted to use the network. The private company was not in the electricity business but aimed to hang its own lightweight cables from the existing poles and pylons and to use existing underground ducts.

When approached, the electricity company virtually ignored the enquiry, simply because they had never envisaged such an arrangement. A new approach was made, spelling out the attractions of the offer in somewhat more detail.

With still no response, because nobody quite knew who should handle the matter or how, the potential partner was moved to give more and more details of the offer, indicating the benefits and the longer term potential for joint working.

After two or three efforts had been made to open the negotiating door, the electricity company suddenly decided that it was a serious proposal and that they should show interest. They wrote to their suitor indicating that they were prepared to discuss the opportunities. By then, the private company had become rather annoyed and frustrated at being ignored so they:

- Replied that they were currently negotiating with another organization.

- Put out some publicity, which was picked up by various local papers, that they were about to launch their new service.

- Suggested that, just in case there was still something worth discussing, a meeting should be arranged.

Eventually, the outcome was that the electricity company did reach agreement and sign a contract. The terms were significantly more advantageous to them than if they had dived in in reply to the first approach. The managers concerned congratulated themselves on a first class piece of negotiating and on having employed exactly the right tactics.

It would, however, have been more encouraging had they actually realized that they were adopting the line below.

> **Appearing not to negotiate is often a very powerful tactic**

REALIZING IT'S TIME TO NEGOTIATE

Specifying

We have already touched very briefly on the specification stage of the purchasing process: now let us consider it in more detail. We will take as an example an item of water purification plant required for a new factory project.

The requirement for the equipment arises from a manufacturing process needing very pure water for washing a high technology product and there are a number of suppliers of appropriate equipment in the market. The engineers responsible for the process want to be absolutely sure that the water quality is perfect. To them, this is a simple matter and they issue the best specification they can draw up.

This can be the start of a very worthwhile negotiation process. The perfect equipment will cost the earth and take years to design and deliver – probably far more cost and time than are acceptable to the engineers who have specified it. So every aspect which can be simplified during initial internal negotiation is likely to save both time and money.

Initially the production manager, engineers, buyer and project accountant will have to negotiate to reach an optimum solution. Since all four are likely to have different objectives at the outset of the negotiation, there is a great deal that can be done to achieve a mutually satisfactory solution. Of course, not everyone will come out of the negotiation feeling totally satisfied, but if time and cost are saved and the overall objectives are met the negotiation will have been worthwhile.

Another major advantage to be gained from this internal negotiation process is that the buying team is far better prepared to face the opposition, being well armed not only with technical and commercial data but also with the arguments for and against different contract arrangements.

There is no difference in principle between the type of negotiation on specifications that happens within an organization and the more readily recognized price negotiation between the organization and its suppliers. The techniques and discussion in this book apply equally well to both. Of course, if the specification excludes all but one vendor anyway, there may be very little scope for negotiation, whoever is handling it. In this case, it is better to go back to first principles and broaden the supplier base.

Prior to quotation

The specification has now been finalized and advantage taken of information exchanged during the discussions and negotiations between the buyer and potential sellers. It is now appropriate to move on to the next stage of negotiation – that which occurs before inviting quotations from suppliers. There are still matters to be clarified on delivery, pricing, payment and quality, as well as a variety of other aspects, depending on the nature of the deal to be struck.

The parties involved will now try to establish positions of increased strength in order to influence the quotation stage and the subsequent interpretation and evaluation process. Continuing the theme of our water purification plant, we can see that the buyer and the potential vendors will have quite different interests at this stage. The buyer will be seeking to:

- Identify the most suitable suppliers for quotations.

- Indicate the importance of competitive pricing.

- Demonstrate that concessions may be given, but only against substantial cost savings.

- Emphasize the importance of guaranteed delivery against financial penalties.

- Illustrate the value of dealing with his organization.

- Ensure that vendors fully understand the bid evaluation criteria to be used.

The vendor will be seeking to:

- Be the sole tenderer if possible or to obtain a place on the list of tenderers.

- Feed in the view that his is the only truly satisfactory product.

- Illustrate the advantages of dealing with his company and using his products.

- Indicate why his product is worth a higher price.

- Have the delivery time adjusted to suit his delivery.

- Assess the price that the buyer has in mind and any technical concessions that might be available.

There are two other specific points at this stage that both parties will find it worthwhile discussing, and which either might raise during the pre-contract negotiations. They are:

- The likelihood of arranging future longer term trading relationships.

- Opportunities for the vendor to provide other goods or services, or to supply to other parts of the same organization.

It is likely that at least the initial negotiations at this stage will be carried out in writing as there may be a large number of suppliers/contractors interested in submitting quotations. During both the written and the face to face stages, buyers have the task of identifying which vendors should be invited to bid, while potential bidders will try to demonstrate that their solution is superior. The process of building a bidders' list is known as pre-qualification and should be a two way activity involving flexibility of approach by both sides.

There are two specific points to note from this aspect of negotiation, namely:

- It does not result directly in an agreement between the parties involved: there should, however, be benefit to both sides and make subsequent activities of far greater relevance.

- None of the negotiation is directly about price: certain aspects of the discussion, as we have seen, may be concerned with price, but the topic is not directly negotiated.

It is well worth noting at this stage that what might be termed the 'indirect negotiation', which takes place before bids are requested, can be a valuable source of information for both sides. This is often not appreciated by the people involved, who may thus miss opportunities to strengthen their positions for later stages of the process.

Post-tender negotiation

This is the single aspect of negotiation that raises the largest number of questions about ethics, probity and significance in terms of value for money. It arises after competitive bids have been received but before an order is placed. That is, of course, when the interest of the suppliers is at its highest and the buyer is often under the most pressure to complete a contract.

Until a few years ago, the great majority of public sector personnel held the view that post-tender negotiation (PTN) was immoral, as it was unreasonable to invite all suppliers to give best prices and terms by a deadline and then to negotiate with only one or two. Many in the private sector held the same view, albeit a smaller proportion.

It seems likely that many of those who were opposed to PTN took their positions because of lack of skill in negotiating, fear of accusations of dishonesty and concern about the need to make subjective decisions during a negotiation. PTN does mean that only a small number of suppliers have the chance to modify their terms but these should be the bidders who were closest to obtaining the contract after the first round of tendering. If suppliers are willing to change their offers, why should the purchaser not take advantage of this fact?

As long as the guidelines are clear and understood by all and as long as the bidders with whom negotiations are carried on are not given significant concessions not available to the others, PTN is a fair and justifiable approach.

Opinions have now changed substantially – but not entirely – in both the public and private sectors. PTN is undertaken widely and its use is still increasing. It is interesting to note that the government in the Federal Republic of Germany required its central purchasing personnel to introduce PTN and, in 1985, estimated that it had saved a net amount of around 8 per cent on the overall bill for goods and services.

Post-tender negotiation has been endowed with a mystique quite separate from that of any other form of negotiation and there really is no reason for this. If you decide that it may be appropriate to negotiate with a selected group of bidders – possibly considering the most attractive offer first, rather than more than one at a time – then the tenderers should be informed in the documents they are sent that the possibility exists.

The German government example is useful in demonstrating a common fallacy about PTN. Many people will say that bidders simply put up their prices, or put particularly onerous conditions on their bids, simply in order to have something to give away. Then you may end up with a worse deal *after* negotiating than if you had never signalled it as your intention.

In fact, a well drawn set of tender documents, sent out to suppliers or providers of services that have been properly selected, does not give rise to such a problem. This is a point of experience that has been demonstrated by a very large number of successful buyers of goods and services who have used PTN over many years.

Even in a difficult market, where suppliers are able to set many of their own conditions, the good negotiator will be able to gain some advantage from PTN.

Having noted that there is no particular mystery about PTN it remains only to add that the discussion in this book about negotiation in general applies equally as well to negotiating after receiving bids as to any other time.

• *PTN IN THE CONSTRUCTION INDUSTRY* •

It is normal practice in the construction industry to seek competitive bids for the great majority of the work which is undertaken on a site. Indeed, it is becoming more common for even the professional team of architect, consulting engineer and quantity surveyor to have to bid competitively for their work.

Here, both sides – the clients and the consultants and contractors have developed PTN to a fine art. This is often because there are alternative ways of doing things and bidders may have useful suggestions – saving time or cost or both – that had not been thought of already.

On occasions, bidders may be able to offer very specific skills that are not available to others or may themselves have spent time thinking of an original approach to completing a project successfully.

Here, then, it would be absurd to send out the tender documents inviting bids for one method or solution and not negotiating, when a quite different concept could be enormously beneficial. The correct process is to invite firm bids on the standard basis and ask in addition for alternative ideas together with either firm or indicative prices. Then tenders can be compared and decisions taken as to which of the alternatives might be worthy of further discussion.

Of course, bidders can put in many hours of work to devise novel approaches, only to find that they are not even given the chance to negotiate them. But that is the chance they know they take when they commit the time. It is a matter for their own judgement.

Post-tender negotiation has become a way of life in construction and operates to the general advantage of the industry and its clients.

Post-contract negotiation

Post-contract negotiation can occur immediately a contract is signed (or more simply, immediately an order is placed either formally or informally) or at any time during the contract's validity.

This is another topic of particular interest because many involved in the business of procurement do not believe that it can be done. However, many suppliers and contractors are well aware of the power and value to the buyer of post-contract negotiation and would therefore rather avoid it. However, even they can find benefit from this type of activity.

Where a contract has been signed willingly (and even eagerly) by both parties, there is little reason why they should not continue to discuss implementation so that both parties can achieve satisfactory goals. In almost all contracts there has to be such discussion and it generally constitutes negotiation, with both parties trying to achieve at least a little extra without giving away anything important.

Since this is a form of negotiation, the side that is best prepared, understands the terms of the agreement best and maps out an appropriate strategy is likely to gain more and concede less.

In previous sections, emphasis has been placed upon the fact that a great deal of negotiation is not about price. Indeed, while contracts are running, most of the negotiation that takes place is about timing of events, availability of information or materials, inspection and quality. The buyer wants to be supplied with the goods or services to fit his particular requirements – which may have changed since the contract terms were agreed – and the supplier or contractor wants to take advantage of means of reducing his own costs and effort, as well as overcoming delays which are his own fault or caused by others.

Clearly, the most satisfactory outcome from such conditions is obtained when the two negotiating parties have a positive will to achieve success and are supportive and flexible rather than antagonistic. It is another instance where a positive determination to avoid legislation or arbitration can yield dividends for both sides.

• POST-CONTRACT NEGOTIATION – A CASE STUDY •

In my younger days, I was Assistant Resident Engineer on a civil engineering construction site. The contractor had won the job by competitive tender and was generally felt to have put in far too low a price.

Sure enough, the job had hardly started when letters began to arrive from the contractor's site staff bringing to our attention that this or that task had not been included in the tender documents and was, therefore, to be charged as an extra. It appeared that these 'claims', as they are known in the industry, would exceed the value of the work that the contractor agreed was covered by the contract.

Being young and eager to make my mark on the world, I vigorously scanned the contract terms for ways to throw out the claims and even to make counterclaims against the struggling contractor.

My boss was a much more experienced and shrewd operator. He was disdainful and ignored the claims for some time, only agreeing to discuss them when the contractor really pushed hard.

By doing nothing, he was demonstrating what he thought and, when it came to the meeting he indicated gently but firmly that he was not even prepared to consider some of the arguments. However, he said, if the contractor really wished to pursue his more absurd claims, he would be pleased to pass all that had been submitted on to our head office for consideration. As in many organizations, referral to our head office was known to be the kiss of death – the claims would never be heard of again.

Gradually he managed to sort out the reasonable from the unreasonable; the work on site proceeded satisfactorily; the contractor was paid fair amounts; my boss continued to be conciliatory but firm: relationships between those concerned remained satisfactory and I learned a great deal about the art of successful negotiation.

Completion of contract

Negotiation when all the work on a contract has been completed but there are outstanding claims for extra payments is very common in the construction, process plant and heavy engineering industries. Indeed, there are contractors who would make no profit at all without this means of topping up their bid prices. There are also consultants who make a living out of helping contractors present their claims and clients to oppose them. One technique used widely by clients is to hold back a substantial sum of money that is believed by the contractor to be due. This can be negotiation at its toughest!

There is no sure way to avoid this type of negotiation if one of the parties is determined to bring it to the fore. The only way to come out on top is to ensure that you have understood the contract, kept within it wherever possible, maintained clear written records of any changes and insisted on clearing up arguments and ambiguities as you went along. This has the effect of spreading the negotiations over the whole contract period and allowing each item to be dealt with on its merits.

It has to be said, however, that this structured and reasonable approach is simply not possible in some parts of the world and in such places one needs all one's negotiating skills to avoid the pitfalls at the end of a contract.

WHY NEGOTIATE?

We have already seen that one reason for negotiating is to reduce the prices that are being paid – the West German government's 8 per cent is a good example. But while we are considering the buyer's view that negotiation is aimed at (among other things) reducing prices, we must remember the salesman's reason for negotiating, which is (among other things) to increase the price if possible and, if not, at least to hold it the same. But we have also seen that there are many other aspects in commercial life that can be negotiated. In this section, a number of reasons for negotiating are considered.

Basis of agreement

When we were considering the purchase of the water purification plant, we examined the buyer's interest in pre-contract negotiation and that of the salesman. We saw how both could benefit from negotiation at that stage. In particular, it was clear that negotiations can be valuable even if they are not intended to lead to agreement in themselves, but only to a *basis for agreement*.

A good example of negotiating to find a basis of agreement but not an agreement in itself, has been the Strategic Arms Limitation Talks (SALT). Both the Russians and the Americans were trying to probe the others' views in the hope of making an advantageous breakthrough. They gradually came to know each other better and narrowed down their differences so that, eventually, another forum could reach agreement. The Gorbachev/Reagan accord in late 1987 was the outcome, and depended heavily upon the initial round of protracted and apparently unproductive negotiations.

In a more commercial sense, we see negotiations to reach a basis for agreement taking place on friendly mergers between two businesses. The two boards of directors will meet and discuss the logic of merging and the advantages to both parties. They may then find that, in principle, they could be in a position to agree, subject to satisfactory details being worked out. That represents the end of that stage of the negotiations. More junior people in both organizations will then work out the details and the directors will be invited later to ratify the final terms.

This type of negotiation can save a great deal of time and effort by establishing first that there is a basis for agreement and then defining certain of the parameters within which agreement will be reached. Then, when both parties feel that this firm and fair basis exists, the final, more detailed negotiations can take place with a high probability of success.

The right price

Although other sections in this book emphasize that price is not the only aspect to negotiate, it is the most common subject that is dealt with and is by no means the easiest to negotiate.

Many of the methods, approaches, techniques and tactics discussed later concern price, although they often refer also to most of the other features that will be negotiated.

It is important to keep in mind when discussing price that the object should always be to achieve not just the best price but the best overall *value for money*. It is well known in the purchasing world that:

> Any fool can achieve a lower price but it takes a clever fool to get better quality and delivery as well

Considering that both buyers and sellers will be aware of this, it is worth noting that buyers often pursue all points apart from price before finally seeking reductions and in that way hope to achieve the most satisfactory outcome. Sellers, on the other hand, may well see their most productive path as being to offer a price reduction first and hope to stampede the buyer into an order. If this does not succeed, the reduction on offer can always be retracted progressively as concessions on other aspects are granted.

Lowest price or best deal?

'It's unwise to pay too much but it's unwise to pay too little. When you pay too much you lose a little money. That's all. When you pay too little you sometimes lose everything, because the thing you bought was incapable of doing the thing you bought it to do. The common law of business prohibits paying a little and getting a lot. It can't be done. If you deal with the lowest bidder it's well to add something for the risk you run. And if you do that, you will have enough to pay for something better.'

John Ruskin

The time element

There are five aspects to the time element in negotiation:

- Either party may seek to ensure that the timings quoted in an agreement are to their own advantage.

- There will be occasions when one of the parties wishes to leave timings vague rather than have them stated clearly.

- The time available for negotiation may not be adequate and could put one party under more pressure than the other.

- Time constraints, either genuine or false, are often used deliberately to try to bring negotiations to a conclusion.

- Flexibility in timing can make a very major difference to your ability to reach a satisfactory agreement.

The question of how to handle timing to your own advantage in negotiation is dealt with in more detail in Chapter 5. An example of each of the five points above is given below.

One

A   Good. So, the contract can read that you agree to pay under the damages clause for all loss of production due to breakdowns exceeding three days.

B   Do you mean losses of more than three days or breakdowns? Three man days or factory days? Weekends? From notification or from breakdown? Payment for all days or just those in excess of the first three?

Two

A   I'll get on to that next week as we agreed without fail, trust me.

B   I'm not interested in when you will start but in when will you finish.

Three

A   Look, I know this is a darned nuisance, but if we don't get that plane back in the air in half an hour we'll have all hell let loose.

B   But I can't possibly contact my suppliers and get prices in that time. I'll have to go to stockists and pay through the nose.

Four

A   OK, that looks like just the product we need. But I don't want it delivered until 3 June and I'm not paying until it is delivered.

B   Fine. I'll put that on order. 3 June is impossible – we're moving our warehouse. It's either immediate delivery or mid-August.

Five

A   I know that you will need these at four specific times in the year but, if we could deliver at a steady rate, we could cut overtime, stabilize quality, reduce the risk of a supply failure and pass on some of the cost savings.

B   That would put up our storage costs. But it is well worth looking at. If you could deliver to our three warehouses and take up their spare space, I am sure we could do a deal.

• *ELECTIONEERING* •

An interesting example of the effect of time on negotiations comes from the British General Election of 1987. The Government called an election for June and faced the problem of not being able to pass its Finance Bill before dissolution. This would have had grave consequences for levying taxes and for a number of features essential to efficient government.

Fierce negotiations took place as the opposition tried to remove a whole range of issues and both sides struggled to gain political advantage. The Government had the problem of passing the Bill and therefore had to make concessions. The fact that Finance Bill issues played so little part in the election campaign is a testament to the success that both parties had in negotiating the content of the slimmed-down Bill and preventing the other gaining advantage.

This is a very good example of negotiation, with both sides gaining at least the minimum positions from which they were prepared to reach agreement.

Other elements

There are a number of other elements of commercial activity which may require negotiation. They might arise before a contract is agreed or when it is under way or when it is complete.

We have also discussed internal negotiation related to the creation of annual budgets and certain topics related to purchasing and contracts, and there are many similar instances of negotiation with colleagues.

Some of the elements that might be negotiated internally or externally are:

- Questions of quality.

- Minor changes which benefit one party substantially without significantly affecting the other.

- Obtaining clarification of an aspect of a specification or the terms of a contract.

- Matters affecting the appointment, transfer or use of personnel.

- Establishing information which may be of use in present or future negotiations.

Of these points, it is particularly interesting to consider quality. Quality of goods or services is often difficult to define accurately, although particular features – such as size, colour or weight – may be measurable with little disagreement. Non-physical quality issues are much more difficult to define and therefore more difficult to negotiate about.

Take, for example, the problem of specifying the quality of a security service – one can dictate the number of guards required at different points, but setting out the quality of the service they deliver is somewhat more difficult. This type of question is taxing many people as organizations move towards increasing levels of contracting out of services felt to be peripheral to their main activities. Similarly, contractors putting in bids for such work have difficulty in demonstrating how they would meet or improve upon the quality of service previously said to have been provided.

It is important, therefore, to realize that there is little point demanding a standard unless it can be measured to a reasonable degree of accuracy. Once that can be done, the acceptable variations from the standard can be set, even if these are entirely subjective. The ability to set a mutually comprehensible and reasonably measurable standard permits negotiation on that issue to take place.

A frequently used method of overcoming the difficulty of specifying quality accurately is to ask the supplier and buyer to each produce examples of what they seek and then to debate perceived differences until agreement is obtained. Of course, this is easier with products than with services.

There are two key implications for negotiation in this question of uncertain specification:

- You can spend a lot of time, and give away a lot of information, negotiating something which you cannot enforce anyway.

- You may find yourself swapping concessions and giving ground on issues which actually have little or no real substance.

There will be occasions when a small change in the terms agreed between two parties can have a very significant commercial effect on one, but little or no effect on the other. When this occurs, the skill lies in the party who stands to gain taking full advantage of the fact, while not allowing the negotiating opponent to become aware of the position. This involves use of many of the techniques of negotiation covered later in this book.

Some examples where this has occurred in practice recently are:

- A road haulage contractor who suggested a slightly different schedule from that sought so that he could pick up loads for the return journeys: his bid won the contract.

- A kitchen installer who offered a customer a slightly more attractive price on one range of fittings: one more sale would enable a whole container load to be ordered from overseas at a substantial discount.

- A refuse contractor working for a local authority negotiated to keep the council's depot open during lunchtimes; the contractor was able to eliminate one vehicle and crew because of the extra flexibility.

Even with the most careful drafting of specifications and terms of contract, there can be areas which require clarification once work is under way. On verbal agreements or those on which the minimum of written definition has been given, clarification is frequently required. Skilled negotiators can ensure that the discussion that arises does not damage their commercial interests and, indeed, they may even be able to take advantage of the situation, as in the following example:

The tree feller

A   Well, we've taken off all the branches that you said and I'm sure the tree will be healthier for it. And you'll have much more sun in the garden.

B   Yes, it looks much better now, and safer. How much longer will you be?

A   Well, we just have to get our saws and other kit on to the truck and we can leave. It's taken much longer than I thought but I gave you a price and I'll stick to it. I don't believe in going back on a deal. It was my mistake and I can't ask you to pay extra for that, can I?

B   But what about all the branches and the stuff that's all over the garden? What about clearing that away?

A   Well, it would take you some time, wouldn't it? We'd be happy to do it if you want. We could start on it today, although it'll be dark soon. We'd have to come back tomorrow and it would probably be two or three trips with the truck to dump it all. Let's say another 60 quid.

B   Come off it – that was all part of the deal. I'm not paying another 60 quid for work that you should be doing anyway. You aren't telling me that you expected just to chop it all off and leave it lying all over the garden. How am I supposed to get it all shifted?

A   Well, lots of my clients want the wood to burn. Very popular nowadays are wood fires. Tell you what, there's been a misunderstanding so I'll try to meet you on this. You give us a hand cutting and loading, and if you don't mind us leaving the smaller bits for you to clear up – they'll all go in the boot of your car to be dumped – I'll split the difference with you and do the job for only 50 quid. Cash.

To close this chapter, it is appropriate to consider the opportunities which arise when negotiating to obtain information that may not be of immediate use, but is expected to be of value in the future. Some common examples are:

- Cost breakdowns, obtained as part of a formal tender or during PTN and used later when negotiating extras or reductions to the contract, or when negotiating other contracts.

- General commercial and order book information which enables a buyer to ascertain how urgently a supplier or contractor needs the order in question as well as future orders.

- Technical discussion with a purchaser, which enables a salesman to identify what the buyer has learned and thus which competitors are trying to sell to him.

- Information about where the contract under discussion fits into the client's overall activities; this may enable other opportunities to be identified and followed up.

It is important for both parties involved in negotiations to remain constantly alert to the fact that they can obtain information for immediate and for future use.

They must, of course, also be aware that their negotiating opponent will be bent upon the same objective.

• *TRADING IN ARABIA* •

Having worked quite widely in the Middle East, where negotiation is a way of life, I have always been fascinated by the behaviour of some Europeans and Americans when out shopping. They first visit shops which have prices marked on the goods and then go to a shop or stall with no prices marked in order to haggle over their purchases.

Their reasoning is that at home, prices shown on goods are not negotiable (a dubious point in itself) and it is thus better to first visit a shop with priced goods to see the 'standard' and then go to one where the products are unmarked and negotiate a better deal.

The mistakes here are threefold and lie:

- In assuming that the rules regarding marked prices in Dubai are the same as in Doncaster, Dresden or Dallas.
- In not questioning why the shopkeeper showing prices on goods would deliberately drive away customers.
- In not observing where the local people go shopping and how they go about it.

Clearly, the shopkeeper who shows prices simply has a different approach. Few Middle East shopkeepers will turn down the chance of haggling over a price; they are good at it and generally enjoy it. Marked prices are only starting points. Customers should visit both types of shop, negotiate in each and buy at the best price they can reach.

Moral
Think ahead, understand the circumstances and most of all, collect as much information as you can before negotiating. And while you are about it, make sure that you obtain background for use in future negotiations.

3

Attitudes and style

'The meek shall inherit the earth'

Matthew 5

'But not by negotiation'

Colin Robinson

INTRODUCTION

It is worth examining some of the underlying principles of behaviour and attitudes in order to put them into perspective in relation to commercial negotiations.

There is a basic assumption running through this book that every true negotiator is out to win. That means to gain more than the minimum that would be acceptable and more on balance than is given away. Of course, there are occasions when a negotiator is out to gain *only* the minimum and where that in itself *is* an achievement.

A good example of this desperate type of negotiating arises when a hostage has to convince his captors to let him stay alive, but this type of situation is rarely encountered in a purely commercial sense. The nearest that commercial negotiations come to this desperate position occurs when a company is trying to obtain *any* business that would bring in more than the marginal cost, simply to stay in existence in the short term. While there are many instances where advice could be obtained from this book to help in such cases, it is not intended specifically for that purpose.

BASIC ASSUMPTIONS

> In a successful negotiation, both parties gain — but one gains more than the other

Thus, the assumption throughout is that the parties both have some leeway to change the terms under which they are seeking to come to agreement and that both have at least some intention of changing. Whether or not they *do* change is a function of their starting positions, the extent to which they have each prepared and the skill with which they use their relative strengths.

It is, therefore, implicit that both parties wish to come to an agreement. If they do not truly seek this, then they are not truly negotiating but simply wasting each other's time or showing off their strength. One of the skills of negotiating is to identify when the other party no longer wishes to negotiate but is continuing with the discussion anyway. In these circumstances, the aim may be to obtain information for use in the future or to try to remain on reasonable terms in order to have the chance of future business.

When involved in a particularly complex or protracted negotiation, it is easy to feel elated when a point is won and some ground gained. It is equally easy to forget that the very fact that it has not been easy indicates that the opponent is well trained and that the point you have won may not be a victory but a tactic. Not that one should become depressed at winning points, merely cautious.

It is also worth remembering that there are differences between the buyer's approach to negotiation and that of the salesman. Most books and articles on the topic tend to confuse the two and thereby fail to differentiate the skills. Although some training courses do target either buyers or sellers, they often fail to identify to their audiences both those skills which they will need themselves and the different skills that will be brought to bear against them.

In this book, particularly when discussing techniques and tactics, the positions of buyers and sellers are both discussed. Whichever you are, you should be able to identify points to help you strengthen your own methods and assess those being used against you.

When negotiating in pairs or groups, and when negotiating over the telephone or in writing, it is essential to introduce differences in style and approach. Some of these essential differences will become apparent in the chapters that follow, but Chapter 7 gives more specific pointers on these issues.

The successful negotiator tends to be extrovert and ambitious and have a tendency to risk-taking. Aggressiveness can in many instances produce poor negotiators, who are suited only to beating down and bludgeoning rather than to the application of subtle and careful techniques. Over-ambition leads to a desire to conclude deals which it may not be possible to implement. An overly extrovert character may become more interested in the battle itself than in achieving a satisfactory outcome.

On the other hand, introverts rarely make good negotiators. They tend to a reluctance to imparting information and to drawing it from their opponents. They also tend to shy away from role-playing – an essential weapon in a good negotiator's armoury. This type of reluctance immediately limits the range of negotiating techniques that are available.

It may, however, be a useful tactic to involve an introverted type in a team negotiation to give balance and make a range of styles readily available. During team negotiations, there is less risk of the introvert deviating from the agreed approach, but he is also less likely to identify and propose winning scenarios.

It can be seen, then, that negotiation is a balance with a range of factors determining the outcome. The approach, attitude and style factors that will influence a negotiation include:

- The personalities of the negotiators.

- The determination with which demands are made and countered.

- The firmness with which requests for concessions are handled.

- The flexibility which is available and used.

Awareness of the skills, techniques, tactics and tricks to be used and countered is essential to any negotiator who seeks to do well.

One final factor is worthy of mention before we leave this section, and this concerns the policies and attitudes of the negotiator's immediate superior and those of the organization as a whole.

It is of little value to try to negotiate when you do not have the authority to make appropriate decisions or the knowledge of how and when decisions outside your own authority will be taken. It is quite common for people to be sent to the negotiating table with no flexibility in their own hands and no power to agree changes. This technique is often used on an unsuspecting victim to try to identify where movement may be possible in the other party's case.

Where the person concerned is aware that this is the first objective, the appropriate approach can be adopted. Where the victim is not told that this is the case, the result can be that the opponents are given useful information, and may even be offered concessions that were not intended. Of course, this can also be a device for misleading or unsettling the opponents, but has to be handled with great care and little regard for the sensibilities of the initial 'negotiator'.

When people realize that they have been placed in this type of position, they should ensure that they prepare themselves as information gatherers rather than negotiators. They should not be too sensitive about being used in this way as they may still have a major contribution to make to the eventual outcome.

ADOPTING THE RIGHT ATTITUDE

In negotiation, as in many walks of life, ethics and standards of acceptable behaviour are constantly changing. They are also subject to different interpretations. It is not realistic to assume that one's opponent holds the same view of what constitutes ethical behaviour and honesty. Even if the concept of honesty could be agreed upon, there would be no guarantee that an opponent would not knowingly act unreasonably or dishonestly in order to gain an advantage.

An interesting example of how views change over time has arisen in respect of PTN. Around ten years ago, nobody in the UK public sector would have dreamed of negotiating after tenders had been received but prior to placing an order. This was considered to be a betrayal of the trust implicit in competitive tendering. It was also claimed that, in any event, negotiating at this stage would not result in further savings. Nowadays, PTN is common in the public sector, as it has been in the private sector for a long time. Few people doubt its value and not many now claim that it is unethical or represents an unacceptable standard of behaviour.

The magnitude of this change in attitude and moral stance became apparent with the first publication to emerge from the Central Unit on Purchasing, set up by the Cabinet Office and Treasury in the UK to encourage better purchasing in central government departments. Guide-note No. 1 from the CUP was entitled 'Post-Tender Negotiation' (1986).

But, while your negotiating opponents may have different moral standards from yours, they may also be significantly better trained and have wider experience. Caution is certainly to be recommended when apparently winning points as this may be a tactic by the opponent designed to throw you off balance or to obscure the real issue. This type of tactic is fair game in a business environment. It is just as necessary, therefore, to assess the opponent's tactics as it is to evaluate and prepare your own.

An interesting point to touch upon here – and one which is dealt with more fully in Chapter 7 – is body language. There have been many lively arguments at seminars on negotiation as to whether the understanding and use of body language can be an advantage in negotiations. To see this in its correct light, it is necessary to ask whether it is likely that the opponent has also studied the subject. If so, it is quite possible that the tell-tale signs you are noting are entirely artificial and, while watching your opponent closely, you are perhaps giving away more than you would wish.

> **Body language can be relied upon only when you are sure that your opponent has never heard of it**

Facial expressions must be considered in much the same light. One has only to play a little poker at a good table to discover that betting on what others give away in their faces can be extremely expensive.

> **Assume that your opponent at the negotiating table is world poker champion**

On the other hand, there are questions of expression and bearing that are important. Some people exude confidence in the way they move and behave. Some sports teams spread fear amongst their opponents simply by arriving smartly kitted out and in perfect order on the field of play. The negotiator should remember this and act always with quiet firmness and confidence that indicates:

> I know what I want. I intend to get there. I have a strong case supported by facts. I am willing to be flexible and sensible. However, if I cannot agree this deal with you, I will go elsewhere

Given an approach of this type, it should be possible to take control of the negotiation, to dictate the agenda and to decide when to dwell on a point and when to move on to the next. This may not make you very popular but it is not an objective of negotiation to become popular. If you approach each session with professionalism and are effective, you will certainly be respected.

A final point on the subject of attitudes concerns the difference in perception that might be held by opposing negotiators. In the case of political hostages, one side might argue on grounds of humanitarianism, while the other may seek publicity for a cause. Those attempting to obtain the release of hostages have no chance to win unless they can identify precisely the underlying motivations of the captors.

It is interesting to note that one technique used in hostage situations is very similar to one adopted in commercial negotiating – keep talking to the other party about something or another and try to collect small but useful items of information.

In commercial negotiation, it is always worth looking for differences in the perceptions held by the two negotiating parties. For example:

- A salesman may be keen to put one of his machines on your shop floor simply to gain access to a wide range of production people to whom he can sell others.

- A brickwork protection company may genuinely want to have a showhouse in a new area and will offer a big discount.

- A colleague may offer to help you, simply to gain credibility with a more senior person he could not otherwise meet.

- A buyer may need desperately to place an order because he forgot a deadline again and is defending his job.

- A supplier may be so eager to keep a competitor out of your organization that quite unrealistic contract terms would be acceptable.

Naturally, some of these ploys are easier to read than others. But the key factor is to recognize that your opponent may have quite different objectives in the negotiation than you. If you can identify your opponent's hidden objective, you can often use it to advantage.

PERSONAL STYLE

> **You are not in the negotiating business to be popular, but when it is all over, you should be respected**

There should, of course, be no such thing as a negotiator's personal style. If someone can call upon only one style, then opponents are very soon able to play upon this narrowness of approach, anticipate actions and reactions and be ready at each twist and turn to take advantage of the inherent lack of flexibility and comprehension.

The whole negotiation might then be likened to the landing of an easy fish. Once the fisherman has come to realize that his catch has few tricks and is increasingly predictable, he knows that his supper is as good as in the keep net. The cunning fish will have many alternative escape techniques and, if really good, only gets caught by a true master of the art.

For three principal reasons, it is essential to be aware of the different styles that can be adopted. These reasons are:

- The right approach can then be selected for any given set of circumstances.

- Whatever technique is being used by the opponents can be assessed and countered.

- A greatly increased responsiveness can be adopted during negotiations.

There are four main classifications of style in negotiating. These are drawn from principles similar to those used in what is known as Blake's Grid[1], and are described clearly in an article by Mastenbroek[2].

Blake's approach shows that there are two opposite ends of the spectrum of behaviour, namely the *aggressive* and the *submissive*.

In applying these characteristics to negotiating, it can be seen immediately that there is no place in negotiation for the truly submissive, following an approach which does not set out to win or to gain much but simply to do whatever is defined by others. Furthermore, the submissive person in this context will exercise no initiative, take no decisions and even be reluctant to give advice.

While there will certainly be times in negotiation when *appearing* to be submissive will prove advantageous – although there are surely not many – we have to discount the truly submissive extreme from serious consideration.

Successful negotiation styles therefore arise across a wide range of behaviour patterns, extending from somewhere near the aggressive extreme, across the median position, that is the persuasive, compromising approach, and towards the extreme representing the submissive, yielding approach.

But whether we are aggressive, persuasive or submissive, we can also be either analytical – that is, analyzing each proposal and developing reasoned and logical counter proposals – or flexible – that is, seeking and granting concessions and helping (or driving) the negotiation forward.

A grid, following the same style as that used by Blake and other writers, is an ideal way of illustrating the alternative styles that are available.

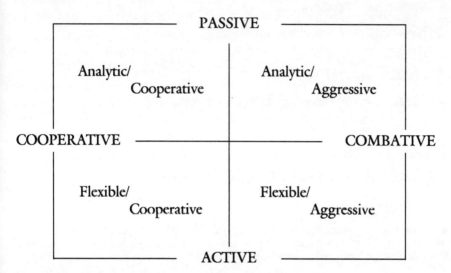

The types described have the following characteristics.

Analytic/aggressive

- Rigorous analysis of a winning strategy.
- Great concern over accuracy of detail.
- Logical sequence and detailed procedures required.
- Specific and clear goals identified.
- Absence of delegation.
- No sensitivity to opponents' needs or moods.
- Becomes impatient with protracted negotiation.
- Totally impersonal.

Flexible/aggressive

- Limited preparation, relatively few facts.

- Absence of detail.

- Prepared to ignore specific sequence.

- Goals not clear, aims high, opportunist.

- Delegates extensively.

- Insensitive to opponents' moods and needs.

- Considers new factors if told.

- Somewhat impatient.

- Negotiation is a personal challenge.

Analytic/cooperative

- Careful preparation of facts and position.

- Concerned about detail.

- Seeks defined sequence of events.

- Aware of own side's needs, wants and desires.

- Delegates but monitors closely.

- Analyzes opponents' moods and needs and tries to meet them.

- Patient as long as progress is achieved.

- Sympathetic but may not be willing to help.

Flexible/cooperative

- Both sides of argument prepared equally.

- Waits to establish details, often from opponent.

- Takes sequence and procedures proposed by others.

- Goals often unclear, become better defined during negotiation.

- Delegates generously, including decision making.

- Immense patience.

- Becomes personally involved, wants to make friends.

Normally in negotiation, the styles adopted will not fall at any of the extremes. Each negotiator will prefer a style which tends towards one of the corners of the grid but must recognize that there is a need to adopt both the active and reactive styles and to move from aggressive to cooperative and back as the discussion proceeds.

Observation of skilled and successful negotiators shows that they can move around this grid with ease and adjust their approach to suit the stage of the discussion, their aims and expectations and the reactions of their opponents.

Such changes of style become considerably more difficult when teams are negotiating. Each team member needs a first class understanding of his role in the team and the behaviour style assigned to that role. Of course, the role should have been selected to suit the individual's own character and preference, but it may nevertheless be necessary to break off negotiations frequently to agree on the approach that will be taken by each participant during the subsequent stages.

Significant changes of individual style will lack credibility rather than confuse the opposition, while operating in a mode too far removed from a natural style will leave a negotiator vulnerable to error.

• NEGOTIATION – SWEET AND SOUR •

In the early days of trade deals with the mainland Chinese many western commercial negotiators clearly identified the various stages in their negotiations such that, as each particular landmark was reached the Chinese would break off, move to another room for discussions and return.

The break could be for a number of hours or days and was used to consider all aspects of the negotiation and, possibly, to apply psychological pressure as well. However, on their return, the western negotiators noticed quite significant changes in the composition of the Chinese team and consequent shifts in style.

On occasions it was clear that each of the Chinese had one style and the choice of negotiator at any stage in the discussions was dependent upon the style perceived to be the most productive at that time.

Unfortunately for the western negotiators, as they were beginning to learn the best ways of handling this approach and gain advantage from their new comprehension, so the Chinese were becoming more skilled at negotiating with westerners and their tactics became significantly less obvious and easy to counter. In other words, the Chinese had begun to understand how to apply their increasing knowledge of western style negotiations and with increasing subtlety.

To sum up this question of personal style, there are three main points to be kept constantly in mind, namely:

• As a first preference, try to keep as closely as possible to your natural style.

- Be alert to the need to change style and react appropriately.

- Take note of changes in style actioned by your opponents; decide whether to react or ignore the changes.

But, no matter what your attitudes, how well trained you are, what your natural or chosen style is to be, or how talented you have become, you must be fully aware of your objectives and prepare thoroughly to achieve them. Questions of objectives and preparation are dealt with in the next two chapters.

The well trained negotiator always:

- Makes the best use of limited time prior to a negotiation.

- Prepares effectively, thoroughly and appropriately.

- Is flexible in defining strategy and selecting techniques.

- Learns from past mistakes and successes.

REFERENCES

1. Blake R and Moulton J, (1969), *Building a Dynamic Corporation through Grid Organizational Development*, Addison-Wesley, Reading.
2. Mastenbroek W F G, (1984), The Negotiating Grid in *Journal of European Industrial Training*, 8. 4. 1984.

Objectives of negotiation

DEFINITIONS

Negotiate

'To confer for the purpose of mutual arrangement'
Chambers 20th Century Dictionary

Negotiation

'The means by which one achieves as near to a required goal as possible using any strategies, tactics, techniques and arguments that are within the bounds of propriety, current ethics and the law'
Colin Robinson

The two definitions above are, on the basis of what has been considered to this point, quite acceptable in terms of commercial negotiation. They could be extended to include the requirement that, on conclusion of the negotiations, relationships should be in place that allow subsequent deals to be discussed. Note, however, that there is already a difference here between commercial and certain political negotiating.

If you were negotiating for hostages and human life was at stake, many people would forgive you for ignoring the requirements of propriety, ethics and law; furthermore, you would hope never to have to undertake negotiations with the same people again. This underlines the differences between these two types of negotiation and emphasizes the importance of not confusing the specific requirements of the two approaches.

In commercial negotiation the outcome is normally satisfactory to both sides. This is not necessarily the clear *aim* of either of the negotiators, but will generally be the case once agreement is reached.

Another feature of the more detailed definition is that it highlights the concept of arriving as near to the goal as possible – it therefore inherently accepts that this original goal may not be achieved. The whole object of negotiating is to persuade the other party to give up some of the ground they are holding, perhaps by giving up some that you are holding. Once ground has been yielded, the points at which both parties then stand may dictate that new goals have to be defined – either better or worse from your own viewpoint.

But remember that, as positions change constantly, so should end objectives. Negotiators must always keep in mind what they originally set out to achieve, but must also be willing to modify their targets as things develop.

Before leaving this issue of giving ground, it is worth considering what happens if you enter a negotiation and neither you nor your opponent is willing to move from initial positions. Clearly, negotiations *can* commence, as the initial task is to probe for signs of just such movement.

But what if there are no signs of movement on either side after negotiations have been pursued? Then, of course, you each have to pull out to reassess your position. You have probably misjudged your opponent's position and they yours. Deeper consideration of the significance of this fact is needed and the strategy and tactics being adopted must be reviewed in this light. If neither of you is willing to give any ground after that, then you simply are not negotiating.

NEEDS, WANTS, DESIRES

Prior to any negotiation, three different outlooks should be considered and defined. Each becomes an objective in its own right.

Needs

The worst case position to which I am prepared to fall back in order to achieve a deal on this issue. If there is truly no prospect of achieving at least this position, I *will* pull out.

Wants

The position which I believe to be reasonable and which I think I can reach with a properly planned and executed negotiation strategy.

Desires

The position that I will live in hope of achieving; not impossible but likely to be conceded only by a desperate or incompetent opponent and with exactly the right approach being taken on my side.

Although the need for flexibility and the requirement to reassess positions constantly were identified earlier, great care should be taken over revising the 'needs' position during a negotiation. It may be modified when new information is gained but should never be reduced because negotiators have become unduly influenced by the search for a conclusion rather than by a wish to achieve a sensible outcome.

A   I'm sorry but I simply cannot accept these terms. They fall far short of what is acceptable and there is clearly no point in proceeding. Our respective positions are poles apart and obviously quite irreconcilable.

B   That is a pity. We have both invested a lot of time and effort in this. If you do not go ahead, you will have to start all over again with someone else and your MD is going to wonder what you have been spending your time on. Are you sure there is not something you can give me a bit of leeway on?

A   Well ... I suppose you're right ... really ... ah ... um ... what if ... so then ... yes ... perhaps ... well ... if I took 5 per cent off my base ... but really I shouldn't ...

However, although the *needs* position has to be firm during the course of a negotiaton, both the *wants* and *desires* positions may be considered as fluid. The more you gain, the more you should increase both these targets.

Alternatively, if you gain information during a negotiation that clearly and reasonably indicates that these positions were not realistic, then you have to change them. By all means move the *wants* and *desires* positions up and down the scale as negotiations proceed, perhaps keeping the gap between them constant, but beware of moving the *needs*.

Should you decide that you have to move the *needs* position, then you did not establish it correctly in the first place and may also have set the other two parameters incorrectly. In that event, the effectiveness of the whole of your preparation must be in doubt.

It is a good general rule that, if the absolute minimum position that you defined from the outset cannot be met, then you *must* break off the argument and consider very seriously whether you really do want the deal on the sort of terms you are then facing.

The melon story

I was travelling through Italy by car. The day was hot and the melons being sold by a young boy by the roadside looked very inviting. We stopped. My Italian was limited to only a few numbers.

ME   Prego, melons, quanto costa?

BOY   Ten thousand lire (Clearly an opening bid.)

ME   Impossible, ten lire. (A mistake, I meant to offer more.)

BOY   Eh! (a stream of Italian followed, presumed to be abuse), Five thousand lire.

ME   (Needing to save face and drive a hard bargain) Fifteen.

BOY   (Bewitched by this tough bargaining Englishman) Twenty.

ME   OK, give me five.

Moral
Don't allow yourself to be thrown off course by the unexpected. Always remember your *needs*.

THE FIVE KEY OBJECTIVES

The precise objectives which you set yourself from a commercial negotiation will depend very heavily on the precise nature of the negotiation. For example, in dealing with goods, one may concentrate on the specification, price and delivery and have objectives related to each. However, in buying a business, there will be issues such as the price, order book, customer lists, stock and personnel over which negotiation may be needed.

In every commercial negotiaton, there will be a number of factors that are fixed and over which there is no scope for negotiation. This point conflicts with those negotiating hawks who say that everything is negotiable but, when specific cases are examined, it is clear that even they accept certain bases as fixed. The point that all things are open to negotiation is worth keeping in mind (even if it is not correct!) as it encourages the negotiator to look beyond the obvious and identify those additional issues that may with advantage be brought to the table.

The first objective in negotiating is to ensure that all the topics on which you wish to negotiate are included in the agenda – but only when you wish them to be.

It should always be remembered that, while you are examining the topics available for negotiation and trying to identify others that *could* be brought in, your opponent may well be doing the same thing. As well as trying to open negotiating doors that could be to your advantage, you must also be prepared to close those that your opponent tries to open against your wishes. *Never* forget that negotiation is a two way process.

The second objective in negotiating is to ensure that those topics which you do not wish to have raised *either* are not raised *or* are countered effectively and discarded.

It is appropriate at this point to consider briefly the various types of negotiation and the different approaches and problems that arise in respect of each with regard to setting objectives.

Negotiations in respect of buying and selling are by far the most common and arise whether handling:

- Goods.
- Services.
- Land and buildings.
- Private houses.
- Businesses.
- Copyright

or a variety of other commercial exchanges and, in all of these cases, the negotiation can relate to major or minor topics that have to be agreed.

But there are many other activities which give rise to the opportunity to negotiate, including:

- Wages and salaries.

- Employment terms and conditions.

- Wayleaves and easements.

- Access rights.

- Payments to creditors.

- Post contract claims.

- Complaints, returns and warranties.

- Out of court settlements.

In passing, it is interesting to note that not only are out of court settlements the result of negotiation but much of the activity inside commercial courts is also negotiation, but through third parties. The point will not be pursued here, but it is worth thinking about!

By considering for the moment only the buying and selling of goods, it is possible to identify the very wide range of features that can reasonably be negotiated. These features will include:

- Specification.

- Price.

- Payment terms.

- Deliveries.

- Quality.

- Commercial confidentiality.

- Warranties and guarantees.

- Service and spares support.

- Fall back position in case of failure.

- References.

together with a wide range of features that may arise in specific instances such as:

- Country of origin or destination.

- Attitudes to discrimination.

- Restrictions on trading with competitors.

- Use of names in publicity.

- Recruitment of client personnel.

- Installation of 'approved' spare parts.

Of course, there are too many differences between individual situations for all to be dealt with here, but some examples will highlight just how varied the topics covered in commercial negotiations can be.

In buying and selling houses, it is not uncommon to come across some remarkably small and apparently irrelevant points, but which mean a lot to one or other of the parties. Generally, the large and small points become mixed and can include:

- The price to be paid.

- Costs of carpets, curtains and other fittings being left behind.

- Responsibility for remedial works or reinstatement.

- Whether light fittings are being left.

- Access date and time.

- Residual responsibility for any third party liabilities.

- Transfer of acceptance of covenants.

- Whether the garden will continue to be maintained up to transfer.

- Locks and keys.

The real skill is to muddle the issues in the other person's mind so that small issues become important and large issues are treated lightly. In this way it can be possible to grant a minor concession in return for something much more important. Indeed, it is not uncommon for people to come very quickly to agreement on the basic price – an issue where thousands of pounds are at stake – but to haggle for days over the price of carpets.

As another example, consider the negotiations which took place between Professor Roland Smith of British Aerospace and the British Government over the sale of the Austin Rover organization. A wide range of the usual commercial considerations took place together with questions relating to:

- Retention of the Austin Rover marques.

- Retention or disposal of property assets.

- Provisions against actions by the European Economic Community.

- Support for British Aerospace's existing business activities.

- Employment guarantees.

- Future involvement by offshore shareholders.

- Relationships with Honda of Japan.

As anyone who followed these particular discussions will know, they were particularly complicated and combined international politics with commercial considerations. It is likely to be many years before the public at large know the extent to which the three key players (British Aerospace, Austin Rover and the Government) achieved the negotiating objectives which they set themselves at the outset. An enjoyable after-dinner discussion is to try to identify just what each party's true objectives were.

The third objective in negotiating is to ascertain just what it is that your opponent expects to get out of the discussion. If possible, this should include each of their *needs/wants/desires*.

Prior to starting the negotiation, it will not normally be possible to ascertain *exactly* what your opponent is seeking as an outcome – unless you employ the most proficient of commercial spies. However, you should be able to make some reasonable assessments and then set out your strategy so that you can fill in the gaps in your knowledge and strengthen your grasp of the weak areas. You can then progressively develop your appreciation of your opponent's needs, wants and desires.

It is essential to reiterate here a point that is highly relevant through-out this book. If you think you know the answer and have mastered your opponent, you can be either very right or dangerously wrong. Thus, even when you believe you have understood your opponent fully, make sure you keep looking for pointers indicating that you could be wrong. Make sure also that you examine every step and concession from the viewpoint that you *are* wrong. *Then* make up your mind. One of the tactics that will be discussed later is to give your opponent false confidence.

Although we have not yet dealt with negotiating strategy, the need to gain knowledge progressively and to ensure that you stay in control of the agenda highlights the fourth objective in negotiating.

The fourth objective in negotiating is to ensure that your own preferred strategy is followed during the preliminary stages as well as when you are face to face.

Your own strategy will need constant review as the negotiation progresses but, if you have prepared thoroughly and if you maintain the flexibility and alertness that is essential to a good negotiator, you should be able to adapt to circumstances. As we will see later, should you find that you have difficulty in adapting, there are techniques available to ensure that you do not lose control of events.

Let us now look at the fifth and final objective that you should set yourself in commercial negotiating. It may appear obvious that you should maintain an objective which is to achieve the aims that you originally defined.

While this may indeed be obvious when you are sitting in an armchair, or debating with your colleagues in an air conditioned, comfortable office, it becomes a great deal less obvious when you are face to face with the opponents in a tough negotiation, in a hot and humid office, when concessions have been fought over and exchanged, when confusion has been sown in your path, and when you are tired and hungry after a tough flight and a long day.

The fifth objective in negotiating is therefore to achieve:

- *All* of your *needs*.
- *Most* of your *wants*.
- *Some* of your *desires*.

Considering the hawks of negotiating theory again for a moment, they will argue that your objective should be to achieve *all* of *everything*. That is an interesting argument but they should then be defining their *everything* in the way we are defining our *needs*. The hawks should then define some *wants* and *desires*, as these are the things that you do not in all good faith expect to win in their entirety.

In other words, whatever your approach, no matter how aggressive or docile you are by nature and no matter how strong a case you think you have, you must *always* define needs, wants and desires and make quite sure that they are balanced sensibly.

An interesting point with hawks is that they tend to gain ground early in negotiations but then lose all of it and more due to their lack of flexibility and their inability to think about what is really happening. Anyone can be a hawk with all of the cards on his side – just try the same approach when the cards are evenly balanced or heavily stacked against you.

Being a hawk, of course, is somewhat different from appearing clear, positive and utterly determined in front of the opposition. There is no harm in seeming totally confident as long as you do not become carried away with the style and lose sight of what you really are up against!

A spaghetti western

In one of Clint Eastwood's many westerns – let us call it 'A Fistafulla of Leada' as it could be any one of dozens of his films – he is confronted by a group of ruthless bandits with rifles who are obviously about to kill him. He has no negotiating power.

He chats to them about a number of issues, unable to identify any that really interest them. Gradually, however, he makes them less certain than they were about killing him immediately and slightly worried about the intentions of some of their own colleagues. Having gained just a little of the initiative and made them lose concentration, he is able to draw fast enough to shoot them all.

He has turned a losing negotiation into a winning one simply because, although the bandits were clear about their objectives, they had not defined and agreed their positions well enough, had not appointed a lead negotiator and had not considered the arguments that might be offered. Put briefly, they had not prepared adequately for the confrontation.

An interesting question is whether, because they felt their strength to be unassailable, they had even realized that a 'negotiation' was likely.

One final point needs addressing before leaving this section. A few paragraphs above is a reference to the difficulty of keeping objectives in view when you are tired, hungry and in need of a break. Some readers probably asked themselves whether a good negotiator would have appreciated the position, realized the dangers and broken off the discussion in order to freshen up, eat, relax, reconsider and replan.

Indeed so. But what if the opposition is in a worse state, or if you really do have unavoidable time constraints, or if some of the opposition factions *want* you to break off so that they can consolidate their position or talk to your competitors?

We have now considered what should be our objectives in negotiation. However, we cannot put these objectives into specific terms until the precise areas to be negotiated have been clarified, initial views on *needs*, *wants* and *desires* have been established and the opponents' position against our own strengths and weaknesses has been assessed.

The preparation stage, which will help in defining all of these parameters much more specifically, is described in the next chapter.

5

Preparing the way

Be Prepared

Motto of the Scout Association

'Those who foresee a danger naturally have a chance of avoiding it'

Aesop
Fable of the martin and the mistletoe

'Nam et ipsa scientia potestas est'
(Knowledge itself is power)

Francis Bacon
Of Heresies

THE VALUE OF PREPARATION

Although each of these quotes is highly relevant to the preparation stage, the last one best sums up the overall objective of this chapter.

Thorough preparation is essential to achieving a first class understanding of what is to be negotiated, deciding upon the techniques to be used, and setting realistic and meaningful targets. Good preparation should provide the negotiator with a wide range of knowledge and understanding on which to draw prior to the negotiation in developing the approach to be followed and during negotiation in selecting the changes to that approach which become necessary.

In this chapter, then, we will examine how the strongest position can be prepared. This must include in particular:

- Collecting relevant and necessary information.

- Knowing the options available.

- Identifying where you have flexibility.

- Evaluating where the opponents are likely to be stronger than you.

- Assessing the techniques that will be used against you, and your best counters.

- Seeing the argument from the opposition's viewpoint.

- Being ready with your own tactics and techniques and suitable alternatives.

- Developing arguments to convince your colleagues that your proposed approach is the most suitable.

If you are well prepared, you can go in to the negotiation with confidence. But always remain aware that you cannot be prepared for everything. It is quite possible that your opponent will have a different standpoint from any that you have predicted, may use quite different tactics from those you expect, and may have quite different expectations of the outcome.

The very fact that you have considered as many options as possible and have argued the alternatives in your own mind and with colleagues, will result in you being far better able to react to and counter the unexpected moves made by the opposition.

• THE POWER OF PREPARATION •

In one negotiation for some expensive engineering equipment in which I became involved with some colleagues, our boss insisted that we plan very carefully, even setting up two other colleagues to play the roles of our opponents. He ensured that we were as well prepared as possible.

In the event, the opponents changed their negotiators at the last minute, clearly had totally different expectations than those we had forecast and used almost none of the techniques to which we had prepared counters.

We came out of this very difficult negotiation well because we had prepared carefully, had a first class understanding of our own case, could adapt to the opponents and had thought around every aspect of the problem. The unexpected difference in the approach taken by the opposition did not give them the initiative or allow them an advantage. The preparation upon which our boss had insisted had proved to be highly productive.

As a matter of interest, I met one of the opponents some years later. He remembered the series of meetings and commented that his side had very deliberately chosen a stance that they knew we would not expect. They were sure this would give them the edge. They were surprised and disappointed that we had been able to counter them so well.

This illustrates one most important factor in preparation. That is, the more options you have been able to consider, the less likely you are to become stuck in a rut or to develop tunnel vision about one or more of your objectives. This does not mean that you have to be easily drawn away from your objectives, simply that you should be well enough prepared to be in a position to decide when to deviate from a certain line and when to stick to it, when to grant a concession and when to seek more from your opponent.

This can be compared with the building of a new road. The highway engineer knows where the road is to start and finish and chooses the most suitable route apparent at the outset. More research is then done and facts obtained which indicate that the terrain forces deviations both in line and in construction techniques. Increasingly detailed design work is done, optimizing the line to be taken and the techniques to be applied. During this final preparation, it may even be necessary to modify the end point to which the road runs.

During the construction phase, further information becomes available, plans and techniques have to be revised, but the ultimate objective is kept constantly in mind. However, if something totally unexpected arises – say rock where sand sub-soil was expected – it becomes necessary to undertake a rather more rigorous review of the whole project than had ever been expected.

One final point about preparation in general before looking at some of the specific aspects:

> **There is no such thing as over preparation – but there is such a thing as irrelevant preparation.**

STAGES IN PREPARATION

Most books on conventional business wisdom take broadly similar lines in defining the steps to be followed in planning. They tell you to:

- Evolve your business objectives.
- Collect and appraise relevant information.
- Develop the strategy for achieving those objectives.
- Assess the tactics to be adopted within the strategy.
- Select the techniques that will be required.
- Identify the skills needed for execution.

Although this applies reasonably well to negotiation, experience demonstrates that there is a much more appropriate sequence and one which gives a far higher success rate to negotiators. It is also well proven in practice that less experienced negotiators benefit from a different sequence, as well as those with a number of good achievements behind them.

The essential difference between negotiation and this conventional business approach lies in the position that the development of strategy arises in the sequence. In negotiation it is best to:

- Define the objectives of the negotiation.
- Collect and appraise relevant information.
- Consider the techniques that might be used to best advantage.

- Develop the strategy most likely to achieve the objectives.
- Assess the tactics to be adopted.
- Identify the skills needed for execution.

The difference here is that the development of the negotiating strategy arises *later in the chain* than does the development of business strategy.

It is worth mentioning at this point, however, that whether in business in general or negotiation in particular, one tends to work through the activities on the list once, and then check back to the initial point – the objectives – to see if there needs to be any revision of these objectives.

In other words, check whether the additional knowledge you have gained while working through the list has thrown light on issues that give you cause to set different objectives. In this way, each of the items can be modified progressively until all factors of any significance have been taken into account.

ACTIVITY SEQUENCES	
General Business	*Good Negotiation*
objectives	objectives
information	information
strategy	techniques
tactics	strategy
techniques	tactics
skills	skills

SETTING OBJECTIVES

We have discussed objectives at length in Chapter 4. It will suffice here to say that, at the outset, it is essential to define the *needs*, *wants* and *desires* that you seek from the negotiation. When the planning cycle has been completed, return to these and review them, make any necessary adjustments and then ensure that all on your team know, understand and support these key points.

INFORMATION – THE SPECIFICATION

Whether you are buying or selling and whether you are concerned with goods or services, the specification is quite clearly the first and most important piece of information which must be generated and clarified during the preparation for a negotiation. It is worth separating our discussion of this topic under two headings, namely the buyer's view and that of the vendor.

The buyer's position

If we assume that the buyer is neither the person producing the specification nor the ultimate user, we can consider the various situations that might arise and how careful preparation can make the buyer's negotiating position stronger. For the moment, the way in which that strength can be used will not be considered. Also for the moment, it will be assumed that the buyer is entering the negotiation alone.

That places the full onus to understand the user's need upon the buyer – clearly things will be somewhat easier in this respect if a knowledgeable user is also present at the negotiation, but only if that user is aware of the strategy and tactics that are to be adopted and of his role at the meetings.

The lone buyer needs to know what the item is, what it does and what the alternatives might be. It is of particular importance to know where changes to the specification can be considered and the limits of change that would be acceptable. One of the most difficult problems to handle when negotiating is to be offered a number of options by vendors but not understand which of them might be significant or worth accepting.

Similarly, the buyer should know the purchasing history of the product or service which is the subject of the negotiation and of similar products or services that could, perhaps, be provided instead of the prime requirement. This purchasing history might include the amount acquired, prices paid, delivery times promised and achieved, the quality offered and supplied and the peformance of the product or service in use. It is also worth knowing the expected future demand by the organization for the goods or services.

To complete the picture, the buyer needs to have a clear understanding of other goods or services that the same vendor might wish to provide. The negotiation can then be opened up to include some or all of these add-ons in order that a better overall deal can be struck.

The vendor's position

There is not an enormous difference between the requirements of the vendor in relation to the specification and those of the buyer. They should, however, approach their tasks from somewhat different viewpoints.

Just as the buyer needs to know precisely what the product/service is intended to achieve for the end-user, so does the vendor. It may be that the only source of this information is the buyer, but most suppliers will make every effort to contact the end-user in order to remove areas for misinterpretation and uncertainty. They will also hope to persuade the end-user to insist on specific features in the specification that will exclude all or as many as possible of their competitors.

Whatever the source of the information, the vendor must obtain a very accurate picture of the application concerned in order to know where alternative features or products/services can be offered on more advantageous terms. Not all of these features will normally be offered at first, but some may be filtered into the negotiation once the position becomes clearer.

Aspects that the supplier hopes to have included may be granted by him as if they were concessions and it is important to be able to identify such opportunities early; only a first class understanding of the usage of the goods or services can give these opportunities.

It has been seen that the buyer needs to understand the purchasing history and this facet is also important to the vendor. However, from the vendor's position, there are two elements in particular that need to be taken into account.

The first is the extent to which that customer has been purchasing these particular products – it may be possible to introduce a new product, do a longer term deal or identify opportunities for additional sales later. The second is the position in the market as a whole – perhaps it would be better not to sell to this customer unless the right overall terms can be obtained, as there is plenty of market scope elsewhere.

The vendor should know of any problems of delivery, quality or performance that have been experienced not only with his own products but also with those supplied by others. There may be opportunities to displace another supplier or it may be necessary to be forewarned of complaints that will be raised by buyers with relation to what the vendor's own company has supplied in the past.

Buyers may wish to invite suppliers to quote for other goods or services as part of a package deal. To match them, vendors must have identified what else they would like to provide to this particular customer.

With a well prepared buyer and an equally well prepared vendor, the act of negotiating can be enjoyable to both without losing its competitive edge. It can also take much less of everybody's time than when participants enter the negotiation with ill-prepared arguments. When either the buyer or the vendor are ill prepared, or do not understand what they are trying to achieve, the negotiation is likely to produce an outcome that is not mutually satisfactory.

●───●

Shoot the Moon

Shoot the Moon is a film starring Diane Keaton and Albert Finney, who play a married couple. They fight a lot and have decided to split up and live separately. Albert Finney moves out. Prior to that they had ordered a tennis court to be built by a local contractor on the orchard at their house.

Faith (Diane Keaton) has forgotten about the tennis court until the contractor arrives. He expects a down payment before starting work; Faith says she cannot pay, although she could, in fact, probably find at least part of the initial payment. She promises to pay for the job at some time in the future.

The contractor is not impressed. Negotiation ensues. Faith merely reiterates her promise. The contractor clearly wants the work and gradually moves towards agreeing to do it. He is undoubtedly influenced by the fact that his client is an attractive woman living alone.

As the story turns out, the tennis court is built but it seems most unlikely that the contractor ever receives his money!

───────────────────────

Moral
Know your minimum position before you start negotiating; keep it constantly in mind. Do not give concessions against vague promises. Never allow personal involvement to cloud your judgement but, if your opponent does, play upon this weakness.

●───●

INFORMATION – THE OPPOSITION

Buyers will frequently talk to suppliers about their competitors – not totally reliable information, but rather like putting together a jigsaw puzzle – and to buyers in other organizations, as well as to their own users. They can often thereby compile a good picture of the vendor's market position, strengths and weaknesses. Naturally, annual reports, trade bodies and credit organizations can give information to top up that gained by informal means.

Similarly, vendors can obtain information about customers from published and restricted circulation sources as well as from conversations with other people to whom they supply.

Where a formal vendor rating system is in use, the buyer can readily obtain data on past performance, but very few organizations have realized the full value of these systems and ensured that they are both operational and properly fed with data. Sales analysis systems tend to be more sophisticated and better maintained.

Further, both the buyer and the vendor must ascertain the flexibility which has been demonstrated by the opponent during negotiations in the past. This may not be entirely appropriate, since it can depend to a great extent upon the style of the individual involved or upon the manager responsible, but it is a reasonable basis until tested or otherwise found to be wrong.

Having obtained a thorough background knowledge about the vendor with whom negotiations are to take place, the buyer must do the same research on all other vendors who are to be considered seriously at this stage. Unless the same information is available about *all* relevant vendors from the outset, the best negotiating strategy and tactics cannot be defined and the opening sessions can be no more than fact finding exercises.

Good negotiators maintain awareness of relevant economic and market circumstances, and experience will provide a good core of understanding about products, opponents and peripheral requirements. Depending upon the size and importance of the order to be placed and the potential benefits, the extent of further research can be defined.

Although it is reasonable to draw upon buying experience, some of the easiest buyers for vendors to deal with are those who lean heavily upon their many years in the business. Experience is no substitute for preparation, however many times a similar job has been done before.

Many negotiators relax when they have prepared as thoroughly as possible and can fall into the trap of believing that the battle is already won. They forget that negotiation is as much about people as it is about facts.

> **The science of negotiation is about facts – the art of negotiation is about people**

There are many occasions when it is not possible to identify who your opponents in negotiation will be. That does not prevent you from finding out about the style which has been adopted by the organization's other negotiators in the past.

One popular technique for discovering the characteristics of the opposition negotiators after the discussion has started is to introduce topics at the early stage that you appear to take seriously, but which are really of little relevance to you. It is useful to test the resolve of the opponents and at the same time have the opportunity to study both the individuals and the relationships between their team members.

This approach is used extensively in high level political negotiations where parties will discuss at great length the shape of the table, the issues which might appear on the agenda, the timing of meetings and the production of almost meaningless joint statements. A great deal of this is for political consumption in the home country but a significant element is to allow the opposing negotiation team to be assessed. Of course, all the teams involved are doing exactly the same thing. The skill lies in gaining more information than you give away.

This highlights an interesting point which is too often forgotten.

> **Whatever techniques you can adopt in a negotiation are equally available to your opponents**

Whenever you can, find out what your opponent thinks of your style and approach. This is most likely to be possible with the successful opponent with whom a contract has recently been agreed. Perhaps over a drink or at any social occasion you can obtain useful feedback. Beware, however, of believing everything you are told – particularly if it is all good! But there are also times during negotiation when you can obtain feedback on how things are going and whether your strategy is proving successful and your style effective.

• *FIRM BUT FAIR* •

While negotiating for some water treatment plant, I had a problem that all bids were well over budget on a project that was itself well over. Some drastic price reductions were necessary, alongside significant improvements in quality, delivery and the supply of spare parts.

In order that we could give final answers while at the negotiating table, my boss was sitting in. He was not known to the first choice supplier and, to create an initial advantage, I decided not to introduce the various people attending – a cheap trick but often successful in a small way. Shortly after discussion had started, my boss took out his cigarettes and lighter and placed them on the table, ready for their inevitable and regular use.

One of the vendor's representatives turned quietly to him and told him that he should put them away because this Robinson bloke hated people smoking in his office and he would probably get thrown out. We then knew that the clear and firm line that I had been taking had been credible and that the supplier was on the defensive.

Oh yes, of course we agreed acceptable terms for the contract or this story would not be included in the book!

INFORMATION – ABOUT YOURSELF

Before leaving the question of information, it is necessary to consider the extent to which the negotiator's own personality and characteristics are of significance and the extent to which they have to be allowed for in developing the strategy and choosing the tactics which will be adopted.

Each negotiator should be realistic enough to take stock of his or her own personality and of the extent to which it has to be adjusted to the tone of a negotiation or subjugated to a style dictated by other negotiators or circumstances. The most able negotiators are able to adopt a wide range of attitudes and to portray a broad spectrum of characteristics, changeable as the circumstances change.

Where a negotiator or a team leader recognizes that this flexibility is not available, then it may be necessary to change the person concerned for all or part of the negotiation. It may well occur that someone who has ideal characteristics for one stage is less suited to another and must be willing to step down.

Apples for sale

A   Excuse me, how much are your best apples?

B   Those there? They come at 86p a pound.

A   Good Heavens, at the shop down the road the same apples were marked at only 70p.

B   Well, why don't you go there and buy them?

A   Because they don't have any left.

B   Well, ours are only 70p a pound when we don't have any left.

Moral
Make sure that the information with which you are negotiating is really appropriate and does not simply have the effect of putting you at a disadvantage.

TIMESCALES

Used with intelligence, the time factor can be a very strong weapon in negotiating. It is worth doing some research to find out how much the other party might wish to reach agreement and what pressures they are under.

• DEADLINING •

An excellent example of the planning and use of this timescale occurred when a customer was poised to place an order for some warehousing equipment.

The customer's chief buyer knew that the preferred supplier's financial year end was coming up and that the new sales director was hoping to produce good figures for his first full year in office. The buyer was therefore rather hawkish about what should be included in the contract price, about the payment terms and about commercial guarantees. The assumption was that the vendor would be inclined to agree rather faster than normal, simply to make sure that the sale could be booked in the current year.

The sales director had also done his homework. He knew that the buying organization (a public sector body) was severely hampered by a vigorous internal audit department and that, unless a contract was placed by the date of expiry of tenders, they would have to go out for the full round of bids again.

Both parties were playing brinkmanship and there was a strong likelihood that no order would be placed, either by the buyer's expiry date or by the vendor's year end.

Fortunately, both sides were capable of being persuaded to be more positive and a gentle dose of arbitration enabled a mutually satisfactory contract to be placed. Had either of the negotiators *not* done their preparation with regard to timescales, one could have gained a significant advantage.

Time pressures can be used throughout a negotiation or only during the later stages to apply pressure for a settlement. There are many ways of using the timescale technique and they must be anticipated during preparation to yield the most benefit during negotiation. Some of the most common methods are:

- Imposing an overall deadline that is credible to the opponent.

- Identifying intermediate deadlines by which certain features have to be agreed.

- Delaying negotiations so that the opponents bring in concessions to start or keep things moving.

- Changing the pace during negotiations so that the opponents become uncertain.

It is an interesting fact that the more you have considered how to use timescales from your own side during a negotiation, the more likely you are to be able to identify the technique when it is used against you. And the more likely you are to use the most appropriate countermeasures.

CONCESSIONS

This is a suitable point at which to consider one of the fundamental principles in negotiating – exchanging concessions.

A concession is anything that gives ground to your opponent. It may be to do with the terms of a contract you are discussing, or it may have to do only with the date, time and place of your next meeting. It may be large or it may be small. It may simply be a piece of information that your opponent wanted but could not obtain by asking.

Concessions and how to use them are discussed in much more detail in Chapter 7. It will suffice here to highlight that, in planning a negotiation, you have to be sure of the concessions you might be prepared to grant and the order of magnitude of the concessions you expect to receive in return. During preparatory work, it is crucial to identify which concessions are important to you and which are not. Then you should assess which are important to your opponent and which are likely to be seen as minor or even irrelevant. Generally, the people facing each other across a negotiating table will not see things in quite the same way with regard to the importance and value of each concession. In planning, you should ensure that you understand fully what you are prepared to give away and what you wish to gain. Then you will be able to strike a balance between the two and decide on your 'gain-and-give' strategy.

LETTER AND TELEPHONE

Again, discussion on how to handle these means of negotiating is covered in Chapter 7, but a few words here are necessary to put the options into perspective and identify what has to be taken into account during the planning stage.

Letters have the advantage over meetings that wording can be considered by a number of people before being put to the opponents, but they have the disadvantage that the opponents can spend a long time in discussing, analyzing and replying to them. Where there is no time constraint, letters can be a useful means of clarifying issues and removing them from the subsequent field of battle. They can, of course, also be useful in identifying issues which are contentious or which need to be subject to more detailed negotiation.

A modification of the letter approach, and one which is useful in achieving the same ends but with more urgency, is to use telex or facsimile transmission. A sudden response by telex or fax in the middle of a protracted negotiation by letter can throw the opposition off balance, particularly where it is accompanied by a credible short target date for reply.

There is a myth that the written word is inherently much clearer than the spoken word. This is true if the word is considered carefully and the writer ensures that every effort is made to assess how the recipient will understand it, but it is remarkable how often a letter means something different to the recipient than to the originator and the blame must generally be laid at the writer's door. During the preparation stage, evaluate those issues that should be dealt with in writing, either before or during negotiation, and those which are better handled in face to face discussion. Then inform your opponent of your plan and proceed with it, not offering the opportunity for disagreement.

The best-known incidence of telephone negotiating is tele-sales, but a great deal of other negotiating is also done on the telephone. This may cover the whole of a negotiation or a small part of something more significant.

Testing the temperature

A   Good morning, Bread and Crumb, Estate Agents, how can we help you?

B   You have been advertising a house in Bland Lane at £115,000 for some weeks now. Are they stuck on that price or would they be interested in a figure around £105,000?

A   Well, £115,000 is a very reasonable price and certainly in line with the market. I would not be happy to advise the owner to come down. Perhaps you would like to view the house? And we are closely in touch with a number of banks and building societies and could probably help you there.

B   No, I'm sorry. The price is too high.

A   Look, why don't I arrange for you to see the house and I will have a chat informally with the owner about the price ...

The ever open door

A   Hello, Mr Brian Brown?

B   Yes.

A   I'm Jennifer Wilson. We met at your interview for my deputy's job last week.

B   Oh, yes. Have you made some progress on that?

A   Yes. We would like to offer you the position ... but the salary you are expecting is rather higher than we were expecting to pay.

B   Oh, what a pity. I was very interested but, if it's not on, I will stay where I am. Thank you for letting me know. I hope you are successful in finding someone.

A   Ah, that is a shame. I felt that we could have worked very well together. Tell me, would you insist on that amount or would, say, £1,000 over your present salary be of interest.

B   Well, I don't know. I see you are willing to be flexible. But I'm not really haggling just to get another £1,000 ...

Many people do not realize that telephone negotiating requires preparation and research just as much as written or across the table negotiating. It is so easy to pick up the telephone to discuss terms and conditions or a potential customer's requirements that the preliminary work too often does not seem worth doing.

Similarly, it is easy to become drawn into a telephone negotiation simply because the other person is on the line and there is no way you can cut them off. If you feel like that, you should give up answering the telephone!

Beware also the opponent who telephones your office and speaks to somebody who is not aware of what stage negotiations have reached or what can and cannot be said. Even cautious people can fairly easily be drawn into inadvertently passing on useful information. All your careful planning can be undone in this way.

Most significant negotiations require meetings at one stage or another and, for some negotiations, the great majority of the bargaining takes place face to face agross a table. In preparing for negotiations, the planner should consider at what stage letters, telephone conversations and meetings would be most appropriate and what means each might serve.

TEAM OR SOLO?

Negotiating in teams is essential where one person has neither the knowledge nor authority to make a commitment on behalf of the organization, or it may be desirable for tactical reasons. In more complicated negotiations, there can be good arguments for changing between solo performers and teams, depending upon the state of play.

Consideration should be given at the planning stage as to whether advantage is likely to be gained by fielding a solo negotiator or a team. This means identifying the skills that will be needed and the people who should be available for the negotiation.

If possible, the decision on who takes part should be taken by, or at least in conjunction with, someone not directly involved – most people do not have a sufficiently accurate picture of their own strengths and weaknesses in this area to be objective enough in their judgement.

There are many instances where both the solo and team approaches can be adopted. Different stages of a negotiation call for different tactics and different skills. A mixture of anticipation and educated guesswork during the planning stage can identify a number of alternative scenarios and teams to suit them. Then, when the negotiation gets under way, a team can be selected to suit the circumstances. Only by thinking in advance of the situations that may arise can adequate plans be laid to meet them – and people be briefed ready to drop into their allotted places in the team.

• 'EXPERTS' WHO'VE NOT BEEN THERE THEMSELVES •

Beware of those apparent experts who tell you of the standard techniques operated by foreigners with regard to team and solo negotiating.

A machine tool salesman who was travelling to Russia was told by his boss – a self professed expert negotiator – that the Russians always negotiate in teams, each team member providing a small aspect of technical, financial or contract input. He was also warned that the team structure changes regularly throughout the negotiation.

On arriving at his first meeting, the salesman was surprised to find that he faced just one woman negotiator and a note taker. This negotiator appeared able to discuss and agree the whole range of matters to be resolved. The salesman, however, had been forewarned and knew that this was just a ploy – he even phoned his boss and was told not to come to any conclusions with the woman, this was the usual Russian opening tactic and a team would soon appear.

Events continued on and off for a few days in an unsatisfactory way with the Russian team not arriving and the salesman getting nowhere. Eventually, and almost too late, he decided to throw away the advice of his boss and start serious discussions. At this, his opponent was clearly relieved and stated that her country wanted to do business with his company but that she was worried about his negative attitude.

She even commented that she had wondered if he had been waiting for the rest of his team, because she knew that the British always negotiated in threes!

As we have seen, the planner must decide whether there is benefit from the point of view of knowledge or tactics in having more than one person present, and how this should be changed at different stages. Some major benefits in having more than one person present are:

- More knowledge and experience are available.

- A wider range of topics might be agreed (eg technical, financial, contractual etc).

- One negotiator can be thinking while another is talking.

- One negotiator can be talking or listening while another is taking notes.

- After each session, the team can discuss the issues and compare views.

- Different natural styles can be accommodated.

As with anything where there are advantages, there are also disadvantages inherent in team negotiating. Some of the principal disadvantages which arise are:

- More breaks are needed for consolidation and planning.

- Opponents may be able to take advantage of differences in view or approach in your team.

- The limits of coverage and authority between team members can become unclear.

- It is more difficult to ask for something to be held over until the right person is available.

- Timescales can become extended in order to suit everyone.

- Negotiators may debate or argue among themselves, indicating weaknesses.

On the whole, it is a useful rule that, the more complicated the issues being negotiated, the more likely that a team will be required.

LEAD OR FOLLOW?

In respect of leading or following, it is again easy to become too heavily influenced by one's own style. The natural introvert may prefer to wait and see what the opponents will come up with, while the extrovert tends to prefer to put at least a few cards on the table and see what happens.

It is, however, more important to consider prior to the negotiating sessions whether one approach or the other is more suited to the circumstances and to handling the particular opponents. It may well be that both techniques will be appropriate at different times during the negotiation and, in any event, personal style preferences will have to be subjugated to the strategy and tactics selected and agreed during the planning stage.

A major difficulty in leading is that the position adopted then has to be defended.

A   We are seeking a price reduction of 11 per cent.

B   I wonder if you could tell us how you have calculated that figure?

Similarly, a difficulty in following is that the opponents have the option of choosing the ground over which the battle is to be fought.

A   We understand that you would like to see some reduction in price but we have already put our lowest figure in our quotation. If you are able to make some concessions on the requirements, we may be able to meet you part way. Now, why don't we provide them all just primed and not worry about the finish coats?

B   Oh, well, er, I didn't think about the painting, er . . .

It is a question of choosing the most appropriate technique for each stage and each person involved. If you wish to attack something, you may well feel that going in against the opponent with great vigour will produce at least a small concession. If you are not sure where or how you might obtain concessions, it may be better to wait and see what your opponent has to say.

It is never right to adopt one style simply because you feel happier with it.

NOT NEGOTIATING AT ALL

This is another worrying technique if it is used effectively against you. The opponent either states or infers that there is no room for negotiation *and* indicates by various actions that this really is the case. It is, therefore, an approach that should be considered at the planning stage. If you indicate that you wish to negotiate, you are inherently indicating that you have something to give in the way of concessions. If you simply indicate that you wish to discuss modifying some of the other party's terms of offer, you may be able to avoid any hint of concession on your own part.

Considering some of the examples above, perhaps the reduced offer price for the house gave away too much about what might be the real target for that prospective buyer. Similarly, if Jennifer Wilson had not indicated anything about the salary she was prepared to pay, might not Brian Brown have had more difficulty in taking up his uncompromising position?

In a complex negotiation, there will generally be topics that you cannot avoid having brought to the table. But, to take the opportunity prior to that to decide on those topics that you want to have excluded and included can give your side a distinct advantage. It is worth bearing in mind however, that your opponents should be doing the same thing and that their lists of inclusions and exclusions will certainly differ from yours. You must be ready to counter and hold your own corner in this respect.

In planning a negotiation, it is always worth remembering two facts of life:

- If there is something that you want to keep submerged during a negotiation, it will somehow manage to reach the surface.

- If there is something that you DO manage to keep submerged during a negotiation, beware that failure to reach agreement does not compromise the deal later.

COST EFFECTIVENESS

One problem that will undoubtedly have sprung to mind by now is that, if all this work has to be done *prior* to a negotiation, who does all the rest of the work in the department?

Clearly, the full range of investigation work is justified only when a significant negotiation is looming and where the difference between the best and worst results outweighs the cost of the effort of data collection. At other times, it may suffice to obtain information that is available readily from other suppliers or buyers, trade directories, annual reports or colleagues who have had appreciable dealings with the opponents or their organization. However, it is always sensible to study the background to the particular contract you will be negotiating and the one or two prime opponents you expect to meet.

It is not possible to be more specific in advising on how much preparation is justified. If in doubt, work through the cycle that has been described earlier and which was summarized as:

- Objectives.

- Information.

- Techniques.

- Strategy.

- Tactics.

- Skills.

Then decide whether the amount of information you have is adequate to support the strategy and tactics upon which you have decided. This process of iteration can yield the maximum benefit from the minimum input of effort at the preparation stage.

• FIGHTING FOR FUNDS •

Having given a lecture on commercial negotiation to some university heads of department, we were discussing the subject over a drink. One of the academics told a story which well illustrated the problems and value of preparation.

He and some colleagues had been seeking substantial funds from an oil company to buy equipment and employ researchers. Prior to meeting the company representatives, they had ascertained all that they possibly could about the company's relevant products and where the results of the research would fit with the overall picture. They were particularly pleased with themselves for having evaluated the benefits which the research might yield to the company in commercial terms.

Their second line of preparation had concentrated on the contribution that they could make, drawing upon their extensive research experience as well as their in-depth knowledge and understanding of the processes involved.

When it came to the decision, they were not awarded the funds.

They had missed out on one very important element of preparation and one of their competitors – another university – had been better prepared. The key issue was what they could offer that was unique, either one feature or a combination of features. The effort that had gone into understanding the product and the company had not been matched by effort in developing unique selling points (USPs) that could influence the people offering the funds.

The next time, said the academic, they would be sure to think through the information requirements more carefully and achieve a better use of their limited preparation time. They would try to identify ALL the key issues instead of only some key issues and many irrelevant points.

CONCLUSION

There are many other techniques that will be relevant in different circumstances and a large number are referred to in this book. However, those discussed in the section above are the key issues that need to be considered and planned while developing any worthwhile negotiation strategy.

The most important thing of all is to maintain flexibility both in developing your own thinking at the preparation stage and in assessing the approach that your opponents might take.

> It is always better to come out from a negotiation feeling that some of your preparation was not needed, rather than that it was all wasted

It is appropriate to finish this chapter with a short true story which demonstrates very well the need for thorough effective and relevant preparation. It also underlines the fact that successful negotiation relies on retaining a flexible approach.

• THE NINE SILLY POINTS •

When I was a young and eager engineer, I held the job of Facilities Planning Manager in the UK branch of a major multinational. We were planning to consolidate two factories, saving money while increasing production. It was a good scheme and, although not my brainchild, I was charged with its execution.

The first real problem was to win support from the workforces, I spent many hours producing arguments, figures, diagrams, layouts and so forth and was convinced that I had a cast iron case.

When I presented the plan to the representatives of the people involved, they listened politely, asked a few straightforward questions and the meeting broke up. I was pleased that my thorough preparation had won the day. Unfortunately, the last man through the door turned and said that, if we proceeded, there would be a mass walk out.

The personnel director took me to one side and told me that I might be a good engineer, but I was far too logical for this sort of thing. Forget facts, figures and logic, he told me, and ask yourself what your opponents will be thinking. He suggested that I start by placing myself at the worst extreme that might be adopted by any opponent. I must therefore say to myself:

- Whatever this scheme is, it has got to be stopped.
- There are deliberate hidden traps that I must find.
- What's in it for me?
- What's in it for my colleagues?
- We didn't get what we wanted in the annual wage negotiations; this is another chance.
- If we can demolish this upstart, it will take a long time before they dare try another scheme like this.
- I can win more friends by killing this than by helping it.
- We'll show them who really runs this place.
- I don't need logic and argument; I'll attack one fact and then nobody will believe any of it.

I went off and wrestled with this unfamiliar approach. Of course, when it came to the next round of discussions, it was not as bad as that. Our opponents comprised all shades of opinion and many wanted to see commercial good sense prevail and some direct benefit to themselves and their colleagues. However, the lesson I learned stood me in excellent stead.

Oh, I nearly forgot. The scheme went ahead and was a great success.

Moral

If you can think of the nine worst, most unreasonable, absurd and illogical challenges that might be made during a negotiation and plan and prepare for them, you are one giant step ahead of your opponents and on the way to winning.

6

Developing a strategy

INTRODUCTION

The great majority of books on negotiation spend most of their pages explaining the various techniques that are adopted in negotiating and the tricks – both honest and dishonest – that may be encountered. They concentrate on what to do when you are face to face across the table from your opponent. In fact, most lecturers on negotiation steer exactly the same course.

The reason is plain to see. It is much easier to produce a stimulating and amusing book or lecture session full of anecdotes and easy to follow tips than one which asks the audience to think more deeply about the subject. But in the real world, nobody can negotiate effectively, and win far more than is given away, without making the effort that has to go into developing a strategy. It is simply not enough to enter the negotiating room armed with all the best techniques and forewarned of the tricks that the opponents may throw at you. It is far more important to have decided exactly what you wish to achieve, how you intend to do it and what options you have if things do not go entirely your way.

The alternative to developing and implementing a negotiation strategy is to rely entirely upon flair and inspiration – an inept and unrealiable way to conduct business.

In this chapter we will examine the principal steps in defining a negotiation strategy and the key issues that need to be taken into account during each step.

In Chapter 5, we defined the sequence of activities that should be followed to ensure a satisfactory negotiation as:

- Objectives.

- Information.

- Techniques.

- Strategy.

- Tactics.

- Skills.

It will now be assumed that all of the preparation covering *objectives*, *information* and *techniques* has been done and the necessary background obtained in sufficient detail and at the right level. How does one then go about selecting an appropriate strategy?

REVIEW AND UPDATE

As the first step in developing the strategy, review briefly the position that has been reached in all of the preparatory work that has been done to date.

Start by looking very briefly back at the *needs/wants/desires* that have been defined.

- Do these look realistic in the light of all that has been learned?

- Should they be changed before you go any further?

- Do they still represent logical and sensible targets?

- Do you understand the reasons for selecting each of them?

- Are they spelled out in enough (but not too much) detail?

and, perhaps the most important consideration of all:

- Do you still wish to negotiate on this issue?

Next, take a look at what you have discovered about your opponents, their views and their possible approaches. Consider the conclusions you reached about their most unlikely and unreasonable approach and what you would do if you encountered it. Make sure that you have assessed as best you can their *needs/wants/desires*. It is a good idea to try to write these down side by side with your own.

For example, when trying to reallocate operating territories between salespeople, two basic lists such as are shown in the table (see page 74) might be drawn up by the senior management team.

Once the list has been drawn up, it is possible to quantify your perception of the opponents' wants against your own to assess and review the major and minor differences that will need negotiation, but always be aware that you are only dealing with *your perception* of your opponents' wants.

Next, consider all of the potential problem areas that have been brought to light while doing the preparatory work and make sure that the principal difficulties that you expect to face are at the front of your mind.

Finally, in this brief review of the preparatory work, you may wish to revise your view of what really is negotiable. Perhaps some topics that you felt the urge to negotiate over simply do not require it or justify the investment of your time. Other points, however, may have come into the reckoning as worthwhile negotiating. And, of course, you should not

---

REALLOCATING SALES TERRITORIES
The Management View

THEIR WANTS	OUR WANTS
Increased sales for myself	Increased sales for the company
More commission than anyone else	Increased fairness
More chance of promotion	Greater mobility between sales territories
New car more frequently	Less mileage on company cars
Less time wasted on travelling	Less time wasted on travelling
More return for less effort (and even more for more effort)	Closer relationship between effort and return
No interference from bosses	Exercise of better informed and closer supervision
Occasional game of golf during the day	Salespeople able to lead balanced lives with families

---

forget those additional points which you feel may be worth using as devices in your overall strategy.

In addition, it is worth bearing in mind those aspects that you do not want brought into the argument and your position with regard to each.

SWOT

SWOT is an increasingly popular management technique for analysing your position with relation to markets and competitors. It is equally powerful in evaluating a negotiating position and is an essential feature in developing a strategy.

Having reviewed your position in the light of all the preparatory work that has been done, you are now able to analyze your:

- Strengths.
- Weaknesses.
- Opportunities.
- Threats.

This can be a relatively simple matter and, if the earlier work has been done thoroughly, need require no further research work. Certainly, the initial appraisal should be done on the basis of information and impressions you have acquired already.

It is usual to consider strengths and weaknesses with relation to internal matters and opportunities and threats in connection with external considerations.

Some examples of the factors that might be included under each heading are:

Strengths

- You really know what you want from the negotiation.
- Your team is well informed and well briefed.
- You know your position in the market.
- You are absolutely clear what your options are.

Weaknesses

- Failure would damage your business.
- The best team is not available to you.
- You have not had the time to prepare your ground.
- You have no idea what might be sought or offered.

Opportunities

- This could start a long and valuable relationship.
- There are other areas in which you could do business.
- Your market position could be strengthened significantly.
- They have indicated much flexibility in their approach.

Threats

- If this fails, so does a lot of other business.
- They are impossible people to do business with.
- If they withdraw, you have no timely alternative.
- You know they have a number of good alternatives.

It may be difficult on occasions to decide between calling something a strength or an opportunity and between weakness or threat. That is not important. If there is a classification problem, it is much more important to have identified the factor than to debate the precise category into which it should fit. The analysis is done to enlighten your negotiating team and not as an academic exercise. Be practical.

Management theory says that the very process of going through the SWOT analysis is informative and constructive. That is also true with regard to developing your negotiation strategy. Once you have assessed your position, it is very much easier to develop a strategy which will build on your strengths and counteract or avoid your weaknesses. Similarly, you can grasp your opportunities and take some precautions against real threats.

DETERMINING THE OPTIONS

There are basically four options available to you in choosing your strategy. These are that you may wish:

- Not to reach any specific conclusion at all.

- To achieve agreement on the content of subsequent negotiations.

- To reach agreement on selected issues only.

- To conclude agreements on all of the relevant points.

It may be useful to consider illustrations of when each of these approaches might be a relevant strategy.

No agreement

This could arise in negotiations between workforces and their management. Both sides may know that absolute agreement is not possible but that the discussions will become easier when circumstances have changed. Neither side therefore pursues debate to a conclusion and both sides can leave the negotiating chamber saying that they are making progress and that worthwhile talks have been held.

This occurred eventually in the factory rationalization example described in Chapter 5. In the end, neither the management nor shop stewards went for specific agreement – both sides trod carefully, ensuring that information was exchanged, plans were modified to reduce objections and the project proceeded quietly and effectively. Nobody ever asked the opponents to say yes to anything.

Agreement on the agenda

This is best seen in political circles when foreign ministers meet prior to discussion by their chiefs at major summits. However, there are often quite separate topics which are concluded by the foreign ministers in such a forum, but not publicized so as not to detract from the main event.

In commercial negotiation, this generally forms an initial stage of the main discussion and may be conducted in writing rather than face to face. Its purpose is to identify issues which are agreed already (or which can be cleared up readily) and those which require the greater time and effort of face to face negotiation.

Where a very large contract is being considered, a vendor reaching agreement on the packages into which the deal will be divided can gain significant advantage over competitors. Hence, debate over the content of negotiations can in itself provide substantial advantage later.

Partial agreement

Most commercial negotiations tend to be of this type in reality, although many appear to be aiming at achieving full agreement. Examples are:

- Negotiations between workforces and their managers.

- Discussions over price and delivery of goods, where either party may wish to leave the delivery only loosely specified.

- Debate over future plans, where it may be preferable to leave some clauses uncertain ('... at a rate not greater than the increase in RPI', or '... on terms based on the original agreement').

- Contracts for research and development, where future conditions are uncertain, depending on the outcome of initial work, and only intentions may be set out.

- Where the complexity of a negotiation is recognized but both parties wish to proceed on a stage by stage basis; here the objective may be to achieve total agreement eventually.

An excellent example of the stage by stage agreement process is the nuclear arms limitation treaty signed by the major powers.

Total agreement

Many negotiations *appear* to be of this type, but actually fall into other categories. It is wise to question whether total agreement is truly in your interests. It is then wise to consider whether it is the objective of your opponent.

There may be no harm in seeking total agreement on a deal and, where both sides can be clear about what they are agreeing, future argument can be minimized. However, it is always wise to ask whether a 100 per cent conclusion is really relevant. But it may be essential to seek total agreement on a deal, rather than leaving specific terms to be agreed later. Some specific examples might be:

- When doing a deal with an opponent who has defaulted before.

- When working in a country where you are not familiar with the custom and practice.

- In the absence of trust between the two parties.

- If subsequent failure to agree could be disproportionately expensive or inconvenient.

- When different people will be involved at the later stage of the contract.

• FULL OR PARTIAL AGREEMENT •

In the early 1980s, when hospitals were beginning to seek competitive tenders for cleaning, many produced very detailed specifications which were designed to enable total agreement to be reached as to the service quality and its delivery. Most contractors (and many health administrators) knew that, although the terms might *seem* to be specific and agreed, it was impossible to measure performance against many of them. Thus the concept of total agreement was meaningless – the terms of contract covering the work quality might well be negotiated and agreed but simply could not be measured in practice. The hospital negotiators thought they had total agreement; the contractors knew they had not.

> **This difference over whether total or partial agreement is targeted as part of the strategy is immensely important**

Unfortunately, in most commercial negotiations, people simply do not recognize that there could even be a difference of view on the interpretation of their agreement. Too many negotiations end up with disputes that could have been avoided with more forethought.

It is, then, important to decide precisely the extent of agreement which is to be sought. It is also worth considering whether the right strategy is for the negotiation to be sub-divided into a number of separate elements, for each of which the extent of agreement might be different. This may be done formally, with clear definition by both parties of which elements are to be grouped together, or informally by either party identifying the elements under each heading but not raising the issue with the opponents.

Naturally, how this is handled must depend upon the size and importance of the agreement which is being sought. However, the concept is worth keeping in mind, even for smaller negotiations, as it can lead to some interesting (and flexible) choices of strategy.

Typical problem clauses in contracts	
PROBLEM	EXAMPLE
Definition of services that are not as clear as they look	Many hospital cleaning contracts
Requirements cannot (or will not) be measured with sufficient accuracy to justify the specification detail	'...will compromise 18mm Swedish timber with veneer as specified of between 0.045mm and 0.058 thickness...'
Clauses that it would not be cost effective to try to enforce totally	'Contractor's personnel will submit certificates of their qualifications for checking and verification...'
Terms of contract that would not be supported in a court of law	Many clauses specifying damages for delay
Agreements that give one party substantial scope for abuse	'Payment will be made within 14 days of receipt of an approved invoice

HOME OR AWAY?

Most people would prefer to be on their home territory when involved in a really difficult round of negotiations. They feel more secure in familiar surroundings, expect to be more in control of the timing of sessions and of breaks, have less difficulty in reaching the location and have information and assistance readily to hand.

The fact that salespeople tend to be better negotiators than buyers, but visit buyers' territories most of the time, is more connected with tradition and the greater tendency of salespeople to be extrovert than with territorial factors.

On the whole, it *is* easier to control events when you are on home territory than when away and this extra advantage should be grasped when involved in complex negotiations.

One of the major values of occasionally playing away is that you have the opportunity to see the opponent's facilities and to assess them. For example, you may find that the organization you thought was significant and well capitalized operates out of a small house and a caravan. Perhaps the offices that would be dealing with your business are poorly kept, untidy and suffering low morale. Perhaps the factory which would produce your order is almost at a standstill for lack of work.

There can, then, be value in playing away for at least a part of the time.

The decision to be taken when evolving a strategy is not only how much to play away and how much at home but whether the stages in the negotiation when playing away might give advantage. Perhaps the initial stages could be on your opponent's ground with the subsequent – decisive – stages being on your own territory.

This is a point which can easily be overplayed. It is worth incorporating into your strategy but should not take on the major significance that some negotiators would have you think. Keep it in mind and select the course with which you feel most happy at any stage.

THE SEQUENCE OF MOVES

As when dealing with any complex issue, negotiations can be handled best when they can be broken down into a series of consecutive stages with each stage being considered separately. This provides the opportunity to simplify each stage, have fewer variables to consider and juggle, and gain a progressively better picture as the discussion proceeds.

It is wise to formulate a strategy which will give you the easiest path together with the least exposure to risk.

The steps to be adopted are as follows.

Step 1
Identify the major issues to be discussed.

Step 2
Identify those issues on which full or partial agreement is to be sought.

Step 3
Assess those issues on which discussion will throw light on subsequent issues or reveal valuable data; these may be major or minor.

Step 4
Assess those issues on which debate will give you a psychological or other advantage; classify the respective sizes of the advantages. A minor issue can yield a major advantage.

Step 5
Ascertain those issues on which debate is likely to put you at a disadvantage; classify the degree of disadvantage.

Your strategy must then be formulated by selecting the sequence in which you wish to negotiate each issue, and whether you wish to conclude an issue before starting another.

Set out your preferred sequence and try to stick to it. It is most unlikely that you will be able to stay rigidly within your own guidelines – and possibly not desirable that you should – but you should have a target sequence and only deviate if you can see advantage.

If things begin to deviate from your preferred strategy, you have to decide whether to stop and take stock or to continue if the balance of advantage is with you.

Finally, bear in mind that you must formulate these assessments in the context of your own knowledge and skills. The personal nature of negotiation means that whatever you decide is the best sequence must reflect not only the principles of good negotiation but also your own preferences, strengths and weaknesses.

• WHICH STRATEGY – PRICE OR QUALITY? •

You are evolving a strategy for selling an item of high quality capital equipment in a fiercely competitive market. You know that you should not start with the price. Your cheaper, lower quality competitors will, but you should quite certainly not.

You have first to ensure that the buyer understands the significance of quality; you decide to first try to meet the immediate users of the product, to whom quality will be significant: you must ensure that whole life costs and users' wishes are the main basis of the purchase decision.

Your strategy needs longer for implementation, but the margins of profit will be higher.

Of course, if you are the buyer, you will seek to ensure that the vendor of the best quality goods discusses price first. You will also try to prevent him obtaining support from users. You have ascertained already that they would prefer the better quality and you know the value that can be put on it.

Your strategy will be to put the salesman on the spot by discussing price until you have an acceptable figure. Then you will seek the quality and other benefits without letting the price increase much, if at all.

It should be clear, then, that your strategy may not require you to proceed first with the issue which is *apparently* of most significance to the final agreement. Your strategy should reflect both the major and minor issues and represent the combination which you assess as likely to yield the most benefit in the circumstances.

IDENTIFYING THE RIGHT TECHNIQUES

By the time the preparation has been done, and the strategy formulated, the negotiator must think about the techniques that should be employed. Selection of the right techniques requires a good understanding of the topics (goods, services, contract terms, and so forth) that are to be negotiated and a clear picture of the objectives.

Of course, in selecting the techniques to be utilized, it is also necessary to know as much as is relevant and feasible in the particular circumstances about your negotiating opponents, your colleagues and yourself. Such matters have been covered prior to this section.

It should be emphasised that the techniques appropriate to any particular negotiation can be defined *only after* this preparatory work. Some writers infer that you should decide what is your personal style and adopt that whatever you are doing. That is both unrealistic and unproductive.

Inevitably, your natural style will influence your approach and the techniques you choose to work with, but you should be able to identify the occasions when personal style is having an adverse effect and move to overcome such problems.

So, the final step in developing the strategy is to select the techniques to be adopted and identify when they are likely to be used. If the negotiation is at all complex, this selection will have to change as you progress but you should, nevertheless, make an initial choice in order to specify from the start how you intend to approach the discussion.

Questions on tactics to be adopted and techniques available are dealt with in detail in the next chapter.

7

Face to face

'It is the wisdom of crocodiles,
that they shed tears when they would devour'

Francis Bacon
Essays

INTRODUCTION

This chapter deals with the techniques that you will need when face to face with your opponent across the negotiating table. It assumes that you have done your preparation thoroughly and have worked out your optimum strategy with care. You have also begun to apply all those facets of your strategy that are appropriate *before* you meet face to face.

Of course, not all negotiation is handled across a table; you may be on the telephone or communicating in writing. You may even be negotiating through an interpreter or other intermediary. There are special requirements for these situations which will be discussed later in this chapter, when it is possible to put into context the various techniques that have been examined.

THINGS TO THINK ABOUT

In this section we examine some of the most significant factors of which you should be aware when entering a negotiation. Some are related to the way you wish to behave, some to the way your opponent may choose to behave. In all cases, the objective is to highlight the most important issues so that you can make a judgement as to which factors are relevant, which could give rise to problems, and how they should be handled.

Stupidity

This seems to be an excellent topic on which to start this section. The technique is to appear stupid when it suits you so that your opponent has to spell out the proposal in increasing detail and possibly in two or three ways. The aims are mainly:

- To elicit information directly.

- To ensure that you really have understood.

- To gain more feeling for your opponent's case.

It is amusing to be involved in a negotiation and to hear a colleague that you know to be quick-witted say:

'I'm sorry, you must think me really stupid. I wonder if you could explain that again. Perhaps I didn't understand the terms of payment and that meant I was unclear about the quality warranty'.

The ensuing explanation will generally be far more revealing than that which was given first time around. In addition, your opponent will try harder to explain other issues to you, whether you asked for the explanation or not.

While it can be positively beneficial for your opponent to think you stupid *during* the negotiation, if that impression lingers when the deal is struck, you have probably missed out on something. Having been determined to seem stupid, you may have acted the part too well!

> Seeming stupid can be useful, but your opponent must subsequently realize you weren't

Honesty

A few very successful commercial negotiators are not honest. They lie and mislead during negotiations, all with the aim of reaching an agreement which is to their advantage. This book does not condemn lying out of hand – but seeks to analyze objectively the opportunities and risks involved.

The deliberate lie can seriously mislead your opponents, can create expectations that will not be realised, or can so confuse them as to disrupt their own strategy and approach. Clearly, this can be to your advantage and, if you have planned to lie, you should be ready to take whatever advantage you can, but, unless you are a very good liar, you will be found out and your opponent will then not believe *anything* you say. In effect, you can no longer negotiate with that person. Even negotiations which are handled subsequently by your colleagues will be tainted with your approach felt to be lingering in the background.

'O what a tangled web we weave,
When first we practice to deceive!'

Sir Walter Scott
Marmion

> Stick to the truth when negotiating

There is also, of course, the contractual issue. If you have lied to achieve a certain contract position, you may find that a challenge in a court of arbitration or law would result in a ruling against you. In that event, you could end up a great deal worse off than if you had stuck to the truth from the outset.

Body language

Many books and articles have been written on body language, generally indicating that it is a powerful device for gaining information. In negotiation, the idea is that you can read your opponent's reactions to proposals and identify feelings of strength and weakness by observing the body movements and other physical signals. For example, I may:

- Lean forward when I wish to make a particularly telling point or when I wish to indicate that I am taking you into my confidence.
- Raise my voice when I am not happy with the way things are going.
- Talk with my hand over my mouth when I am not confident of what I am saying.
- Shift around in my chair when I am uncomfortable with points you are making.

There are many other body language points that can be observed in normal conversation and in commercial negotiation. If you have read the books, perhaps you can read your opponents' signals and model your approach upon these inadvertent messages.

But what if your opponent has read the books as well? Then you have two problems:

- Maybe your opponent is also reading the signals you are giving.
- Maybe the messages you are reading are precisely what your opponent wants you to read.

And there is a third factor which it is equally important for you to keep in mind, namely that:

- Maybe you are thinking so much about body language that you are losing sight of the real thrust of the negotiation!

So how should the matter be handled? The answer is to be aware that *there may well be messages* from body language but they must be supported by other more substantive signals from the progress of the negotiation. Similarly, you should be careful of giving things away inadvertently by your own body language indicators, but you could certainly try to use those indicators marginally to your own advantage.

Perhaps the best approach is simply to be sufficiently aware of the problem to avoid giving away anything significant yourself.

> Beware of body language from either side in a negotiation

Exultation and panic

It is always worth remembering that a negotiation is not complete until every detail is agreed and confirmed. Even then you have to bear in mind that you may have missed something. That is not to say that you should not enjoy the interim victories and regret the interim defeats but it does suggest that you should not make too much of them.

If you spot an exultant negotiator as your opponent, you should be ready to turn this to advantage. Genuinely exultant people are off their guard. If you then look unhappy, drop your shoulders (body language!) and grunt that you 'suppose that this means . . .' you may well find that the point is accepted rather too quickly by your opponent.

Similarly, if you have won a few points, you may find that your opponent is beginning to panic. In that case, ram home the advantage and press for agreement on your own terms. But beware – perhaps your opponent is a fisherman and is playing with you. Is the exultation or panic you see genuine or simply a device to put you off guard? If you can play these games, so can your opponent.

'But being too happy in thine happiness . . .'

John Keats
Ode to a Nightingale

> **Don't permit yourself exultation or panic until the job is done**

Moods and attitudes

This is an appropriate point at which to look at the way your opponent is reacting generally to your side of the negotiation. Everyone has good days and bad days. The best negotiators can cover up the variations to some extent, but not entirely. But apart from the purely personal factors, there may also have been a change in your opponent's attitude towards this particular deal, brought about by factors of which you cannot be aware. Always ask yourself:

- Can I take advantage of this opponent's mood-of-the-day?
- Has there been a change of attitude towards this negotiation and what is the significance?
- Am I being lead up a path that my opponent wishes me to follow?

But, as with all the points covered in this section, you should also examine your own position. Are you giving anything away by your current mood or attitude towards the negotiation?

> **Moods and apparent changes of attitude can be used by you or against you**

Could you apparently give something away by deliberately displaying specific mood/attitude characteristics? Again, beware of being so clever in this respect that you lose sight of your real objective.

Conceit

If you pride yourself on being a good negotiator, you are probably not! The good negotiator is always aware that there are new or unforeseen tricks and techniques which need countering. The good negotiator is also aware that no matter how intensive and thorough the preparation and strategy, there will always be unexpected twists and turns to be dealt with.

• I ALREADY KNOW ALL THIS •

I was lecturing on negotiating skills to a small group and one man in the audience clearly thought he was the best and resented being sent on the course by his boss. He was unhelpful and did not bother to contribute to the success of the course. Towards the end of the day, I asked for a volunteer to describe his/her own negotiating style and have it discussed by the group – I knew who would come forward. There was a gentle but firm analysis by the group and it was clear that the volunteer victim was uncomfortable at the views expressed, although he held to the last that he was red hot at the job and nobody else really understood what they were talking about.

About two weeks later, I received a phone call from the victim's boss who said that he didn't know how I had done it but, for the first time ever, the man was discussing negotiation approaches and options with colleagues before meeting his opponents. I must admit that I did not let on that the improvement was the result of work by his co-students rather than by me.

> Once you know for sure that you are a brilliant negotiator, the time has come to hand over to somebody else!

Mistakes

The deliberate mistake – whether made by you or your opponent – is not significantly different from a lie. It is meant to mislead by giving false information. The main difference in practical terms between the mistake and the lie is that the mistake is corrected later, perhaps at a point in the negotiation when advantage has been gained and it is difficult to go back.

'Oh, that's a very good point. Did I really say that we manufacture all our own spares? How silly of me. Of course we don't. The baffles are made in the Gdansk shipyard in Poland'

or

'Ah, is that Mr Smith? Good. On this draft contract that you have sent, it says that you will supply to the BC469/23D specification. I have been clear throughout that we need BC469/26E, which of course includes the higher grade material with certification. I'm assuming that you have made a mistake and am changing the spec number and putting the signed contract in the post to you today.'

Deliberate mistakes are dishonest and should be treated as such: either throw out those potential business partners altogether – they might try the same trick again – or insist on some significant concession against the mistake.

'Gdansk, ah, I see. Tell you what. Take out the spares and we will have them made in our own workshops. Reduce the price by 18 per cent to allow for the spares costs and all our extra storage and admin and the business is yours'

or

'Oh, 26E. Well, my notes clearly indicate that you asked for BC469/23D. Twice. There will be an extra 8 per cent on the price plus a fixed charge of £3000 and the delivery date goes back by four weeks ... unless you are willing to pay an acceleration charge?'

The advice to a negotiator who intends to use the deliberate mistake as a device is very much the same as that given above to the prospective liar. You stand a very good chance of being found out and an even better chance of not finding anyone with whom to do business in the future.

> **The deliberate mistake may be more of a mistake than you had believed**

The switch

Another dishonest device that is quite common, the switch, requires your opponent to believe that you have every intention of providing or doing what you say. You may well start by believing quite sincerely in what you are offering but then be caught out by circumstances.

You may, for example, sell cars. Your customer wants the Fastback in Altantic Gold with sunroof for delivery in 10 days. You are not at all sure that you can get hold of exactly that model. The contract is signed but, when you try to obtain the car, as you expected, it is not available in time. Others are. You now try to persuade the customer that what you have available is equally desirable.

But what if you are the customer? You have cause to be annoyed.

Have you been conned or was it an innocent mistake? Did you really want only the model described and no alternative? In any event, ask yourself whether there is an advantage to be gained from the switch. What about a discount for accepting what you didn't want? What about some free extras? What about a better price for your old car?

There is another type of switch that is more open and honest. That requires you to try to change your opponent's mind about what seemed to be wanted. The aim is to put you in a stronger position, either because you are the only person who can meet the new requirement or because you could not anyway meet the previous need. Such a switch has to be thought out during the preparation stage and depends upon having an appropriate strategy. But no matter how well you have prepared your position, the competent opponent faced with a switch is very likely to seek a significant concession in return.

> **If you plan a switch, be prepared for demands for concessions**

Confusion

In a complex negotiation, particularly where a range of issues is being discussed and positions changed, there may well be confusion in your mind as to where you have reached. Many people will tell you to withdraw immediately and clarify everything before returning to the negotiating table, but what if your opponents are equally confused? Or even more confused?

If you have been driving the negotiation according to your plan and dictating the agenda and issues covered, you may well be clearer than your opponents about where you stand. In that case there might be advantage in continuing.

In general, however, a confused negotiatior will end up worse off than if time had been taken for clarification. Deliberately using confusion and uncertainty as a device in negotiation can be very powerful as a tactic but also carries very high risks. Similarly, if it appears to be used against you, trying to take advantage of that situation will probably leave you worse off.

One approach that can arise in this respect is the snow job. Here, one party inundates the other with so much information that it is quite impossible to assimilate it. Hidden in the wealth of data will be one or two significant items that you really should know about. If you find yourself in this position, the best approach is to ask your opponent to summarise the significant points so that you can continue. Then, when you have reached agreement on those points, make sure that you do not use the snow job paperwork as your basis of agreement.

'Thank you for letting me have all this information about your products and terms and conditions of sale. Some of it does seem relevant to what we are discussing. Perhaps I might pass it back to you to extract those parts which bear directly on what we are discussing. Meanwhile, I have asked my buyer to bring a copy of the standard terms on which we do business.'

Lack of clarity arising from confusion, however caused, may end up not benefiting anybody when a deal is agreed. It is possible that both parties will discover that they have a contract they do not care for. That is never the basis of good business.

> **If you are confused, step back, examine the position and decide how much you stand to lose; if your opponent is confused, by all means extract advantage from the situation**

Proactive or reactive

There are many negotiators who believe that they should cultivate either a proactive or reactive style because that is best suited to their own personality. In other words, they should either set the pace and define precisely the issues being discussed or should sit back and wait for issues to be tabled by their opponent.

> **Neither the proactive nor the reactive technique is correct**

As with so many aspects of negotiation, it is a matter of horses for courses. Whereas one's personal characteristics will determine the approach which one prefers, this has to be tempered with a recognition that character traits have to be subjugated to the needs of the moment. If the aggresive negotiator finds himself in circumstances that require docility, then docility should become quite natural.

In looking at the range of techniques discussed below, it will be clear that some are designed more for the proactive type and others for the reactive. The choice should be made initially during the planning stage and be kept under review throughout the negotiation until full agreement has been confirmed.

The most important thing to have in mind is that the choice between being proactive or reactive should be considered as a selection of tactics rather than personal preference. We are, of course, generally better at the things we prefer doing but this question is too important to be decided simply

> **There is no such thing as proactive or reactive, there is only proactive _and_ reactive, but at different stages**

on that basis. Training in negotiation should make people able to adopt exactly the opposite approach to that which they feel is natural to them.

Recording

Unless you have a quite remarkable memory, you will need to keep notes of the points that have been agreed and those that have not during a negotiating session. Even with a remarkable memory, you are likely to benefit from keeping a record because your opponent will then be aware that there is little or no scope for suggesting a different outcome.

There is one further advantage in keeping good notes and of being seen to do so. This is that when you confirm the agreement, your opponent may not quite remember which points actually were agreed and which were not. Although this is not likely to allow you to simply write in a point of great significance, it can enable many small details to be finalised in the form that you would like them, each being below the threshold at which the opponent will raise objections.

Of course, you should be aware that, if you are not the person confirming the deal, you should check your notes very carefully to see if there are points of agreement inserted with which you are not entirely happy.

'Forget not. In thy book record their groans ...'

John Milton
Massacre in Piedmont

> The negotiator who has a good record of events has the stronger position at the conclusion

USEFUL TECHNIQUES

We will now look at some specific techniques that should form part of your portfolio, to be taken out and used in appropriate circumstances. All of these techniques should be reviewed when selecting a negotiation strategy. Their use will depend somewhat less upon your own skills and abilities than upon the particular negotiation into which you are entering.

By all means try something which is new to you but make sure that, if not successful, you have not jeopardized something worthwhile. The negotiator can only improve personal skills by trying new methods, but has to maintain a high enough success rate to be in a position to negotiate again!

We will start with some techniques that everyone can use, and then move on to others that need more skill and experience and which should be used only with a great deal of care and forethought.

Biting and nibbling

The first of these two techniques, biting, requires you to demand a large concession and hope that the opponent will only be able to argue you back part of the way. The theory is that, had you gone for less at the outset, you would not have achieved such a good deal. It is not essential to state how much you are biting – it may suffice to indicate that the bite is a big one.

'I'll admit that we'd love to supply all 700 cars but not at the price you are seeking. Let me be quite frank with you. The discount you have mentioned is nonsense. I would be willing to look at 7 per cent in some circumstances, but not 23 per cent. And the servicing charges have to go up by at least 18 per cent to be worth considering. The market is very buoyant at the moment and that sort of discount is simply not available. Everybody is selling whatever they can get hold of.'

or

'I understand that you had been hoping to supply the small computers that we are installing in our branches. Well, I have your price list and discount structure and am phoning to say that there is just no chance. We have tenders from some of the biggest outfits and they are miles below you. But, if you thought it worthwhile looking at it again ...'

When biting, beware of being so greedy that your opponent does not feel that there is any chance of the two viewpoints meeting. You do not wish to frighten away prospective suppliers or buyers with this approach – it would be much easier to tell them simply that you are no longer interested. The bite should be just so big that the other person feels that the deal could still be on.

The second of these techniques – nibbling – means moving forward through a negotiation in very small steps, identifying, discussing and agreeing each in turn. The objective is to obtain a series of agreements where no point on its own would be sufficient to encourage your opponent to argue but which, when taken in aggregate, amount to a very good deal for you.

Nibbling may be done by taking a list of topics and working through them progressively, or nibbles can be made at various times in a negotiation, interspersed with more significant points.

'Good, it looks as if we will be taking the 700 cars on that basis. But on those terms I would want to throw in the colour options so that the users retain a say in what they are driving. And the driver and front passenger mats ...'

or

'It looks as if we are near to agreement on these computers. We should be in a position to accept your idea of a three year contract and the main terms we have agreed. Deliveries would have to be free to each of our locations and we must know that you can supply replacement computers in case of breakdown. In fact, let's say you will keep one at each location for when it's needed? ... Good. And free starter packs of discs and stationery ...'

With both nibbling and biting, a great deal depends on the background research you have done and your knowledge of the market in which you are operating. The more you know, the more you will gain from a careful application of these techniques. You can, of course, bite first and then nibble, but it is difficult to nibble first and then bite.

> **Biting and nibbling can be good for you, but being too greedy can lose you the meal**

Cherry picking

There are mixed views about cherry picking. Some say that it is unfair or even unethical. Others say it is a perfectly acceptable technique in a tough commercial world.

Cherry picking is a buyer's device and means taking the best elements from the deals offered by various vendors, combining them and offering the resulting contract terms to whichever bidder seems most likely to accept. It can thus form a second stage of post-bid negotiation. You receive bids, negotiate with a small number of suppliers and then cherry pick.

Some buyers use cherry picking in preference to market research and preparation. They simply put out a tender document and see what comes in. Then they may go into two or three rounds of cherry picking and, in this way, let the suppliers do most of their work for them.

In the buying of services, the technique is used to produce the detailed specification, terms and conditions. The method is the same – take all the bids and design your own contract document from them.

Clearly, there can be occasions when the method is reasonable – for example, vendors' bids may provide information that you had not discovered in your research or may suggest an improved form of contract from that which you had envisaged. Then it is sensible to use the additional knowledge to your own advantage.

> **Cherry picking has a place in negotiation but not as a substitute for buyer preparation**

Cherry picking is used unreasonably when vendors are asked to do the buyer's job with no intention of paying them. It is also unreasonable when the device is used to develop a contract to be placed with the supplier who had been favoured from the start. In that event, the other bidders, who had no chance of winning the order, have been used simply to define the terms for the preferred supplier.

Presumption

'That which is taken for granted; confidence grounded on something not proved'
Chambers 20th Century Dictionary

Presumption in commercial negotiation is accurately defined in this way. The technique is put into practice generally towards the end of a negotiation, or when confirming in writing. A number of issues may not have been discussed at all, or may have been discussed but not finalized. You then summarise the agreement, inserting terms which have not been agreed but in the form you require. You state them clearly and, if your opponent does not object, they are agreed.

Presumption depends on keeping good notes. If you know what was not agreed, but also know about the differences which were outstanding, you can pitch your confirmation at just the right level to obtain both advantage and the agreement of your opponent. This may be done across the table or in writing. In fact, many negotiators leave such points quite intentionally until they are providing written confirmation. They argue that the other party is less likely to haggle when they see that the contract is about to be completed. Both buyers and vendors can presume, but the greatest opportunity to do so lies in the hands of the negotiator who takes the initiative in summing up the deal that has been struck.

Beware of this technique being used against you. It is not only a device for gaining marginal advantage but can be used quite deliberately by leaving aside negotiation of contract conditions that could prove unacceptable if they were highlighted. When the written terms arrive, hidden somewhere are these very points. Presumption is, of course, inherent in the snow job technique described above in the section on confusion in negotiation.

> **Presume if you will, but make sure you have the situation under control**

Interruptions

One of the objectives during a negotiation is to obtain information from your opponent. That information may then prove useful in concluding the current deal or in a subsequent negotiation. One of the best ways to stop someone giving you information is to interrupt. So a golden rule in negotiation is

Don't interrupt!

But this can lead to difficulties and, in common with most golden rules of negotiation, needs to be tempered with some common sense. Clearly, you will have to identify when your opponent is simply waffling pointlessly and should then interrupt to divert the discussion back to something worthwhile. As a matter of interest, when faced with what seems to be a valueless monologue, you might ask yourself if the person is trying to obscure something, but if anything potentially valuable is coming across the table, bear with it and listen.

The parallel point to not interrupting arises when we consider what you should do if you are interrupted. Here there are two aspects to consider, namely:

- Was the interruption designed to disrupt your flow of thought or your summary of an agreement?

- Does your opponent have a genuine point to raise and are you about to learn something useful?

An interruption designed to divert you must be dealt with firmly so that you can continue. If you cannot overcome the interruption immediately, make sure that you note down the point which you had reached and continue when the intervening problem has been resolved. Never become frustrated about the diversion and never look impatient or angry. When you start again, refer back to the last *completed* point – but do not repeat the details – and then move on. Start the interrupted topic again.

'Now, let me take up where I left off. I had covered the issue of overtime payments and had started on clothing allowances. The first topic was the amount of the allowance . . .'

An apparently accidental or careless interruption caused by events outside your control should be dealt with in much the same way. It *may* have been created deliberately but you should not worry about that at the time. It will be interesting to speculate later as to the cause but, whatever the reason, the interruption should not affect your ability to achieve the main objective.

There will, of course, be occasions when you have little or no control over the circumstances and have to yield, although you know that the interruption is deliberate and potentially against your interests.

'I stop you there, Comrade Smith. I have meeting with the First Secretary and must break off. The Kremlin guard will call your car for you. We meet tomorrow at 8 o'clock.'

or

'Er, sorry, can I interrupt ... I really have to pop out to the toilet'.

If the interruption is made in order to raise a genuine point, it should be dealt with quite differently. Perhaps you will gain information or the point that you were making was misunderstood, incorrect, unacceptable or incomprehensible. Then, to have refused to give way to the opponent would be a bad practice and possibly even foolish.

At times, you will not be able to tell which type of interruption is being thrown at you. In such cases, the best course is to wait and see, making sure that you know precisely the stage which you had reached. Then, when you have decided how to react to the event, you are able to remain adequately in control of the proceedings.

> **Don't interrupt and, if interrupted, learn what you can but don't lose control**

Concessions

First, let us consider what a concession is in commercial negotiation. It means changing a position (which may or may not have been indicated to the opponent) in order to move nearer to agreement. It does not *always* mean yielding to a demand and giving something away – it is possible to grant a concession sought by your opponent that actually enhances your position.

Many writers and lecturers treat concessions as the very core of negotiation. It is important, however, to see the technique of giving and gaining concessions as simply one technique among many.

There are four underlying principles to be kept in mind with regard to concessions. These might be taken as the golden rules of concession swapping. They are:

> **Always gain more concessions than you give**
> **Always gain bigger concessions than you give**
> **Always make your concession look more significant than it is**
> **Always be certain that you can enforce concessions gained**

It is important to know well in advance the flexibility of your position and the concessions on which you are prepared to negotiate. During your preparatory work, you may not be able to align every concession that you hope to obtain with one that you might be willing to grant.

You should therefore develop two lists, one showing concessions you would be prepared to grant and one covering those to be sought from the opponents. Some items on the two lists should relate directly to each other and be seen as possible trade-offs, but others will have to stand alone until the negotiation is under way and your opponent's position becomes clearer.

It is quite usual to indicate that you are interested in swapping concessions in order to aid movement towards agreement. There is no harm in this if you have balanced the concessions correctly. You should also seek a specific concession while conceding only a willingness to discuss another issue. Beware, though, that the issue on which you are yielding does not have more potential than that which you are attacking. Beware also that in your haste to grab at a concession, you have not taken hold of something that has no real substance.

'We do seem to be getting ourselves bogged down in this, don't we? Can we perhaps do a deal? I am willing to be flexible on the question of spare parts but would want the 3 per cent from you on financing costs.'

or

'Yes, of course, no problem. I could certainly put you on our list of approved suppliers. But not unless you are far more competitive on this contract.'

You might be offered a concession that was unexpected or which seems on the face of things to be rather generous. Here it is wise to be both suspicious and cautious. Work on the assumption that nobody gives away something for nothing and few people willingly trade something for its equal, but, having said that, do not miss the occasional concession which is just what it seems – generous and worth taking.

Something which is a bargain to you may mean relatively little to your opponent. Perhaps to your opponent it means nothing at all. Some examples are:

- A contractor who intends to take a price reduction that he has conceded out of the money to be paid to a sub-contractor.

- A relaxation of a delivery lead time imposed on a supplier, which did not affect the project's critical path.

- The offer of cheap airline tickets as part of a deal, but only on aircraft which would have had empty seats.

On the other hand, it may be that the concession that you appear to be gaining is somewhat hollow. Perhaps it will not result in any difference in practice. Some negotiators will agree to pay invoices more quickly than their standard terms specify, but know that there will be no difference in practice. Others may promise a delivery date that the customer wants, in full knowledge that it will not be met.

If you trade concessions, make sure that what you gain is substantive and can be enforced. Otherwise it is no concession and you may be trading something worthwhile for nothing. Alternatively, ensure that the concession which you grant is locked in to that which you have gained.

'Yes, I am quite willing to pay the extra 1.5 per cent for the guaranteed delivery and replacement within 24 hours of any rejected items. Let us note that all of the extra is forfeited if you fall down only once on that, shall we?'

Finally on this question, always try to assess what any particular concession in your armoury might be worth to your opponent. Perhaps you are a buyer who is placing an order far later than you should. You need the goods immediately; you know that your supplier will shortly have to lease another warehouse but that you have space available:

'No, I would have no objection to taking immediate delivery. But we would expect to be invoiced only on the schedule we have agreed. And I would have to ask for that extra 5 per cent to cover our extra storage costs.'

Or perhaps you are the supplier and realize that the buyer is in a difficult position.

'I do wish you had raised this sooner. I could have pushed an order through for you. Tell you what – leave it to me. I'll do everything I can to get them to you in three days, but it's going to cost the extra 5 per cent, I'm afraid. Another thing, it would help a lot if I could go back to my Sales Director with the order for the whole quantity. Then he'd be willing to pull out all the stops.'

There is nothing unethical about taking advantage of commercial knowledge fairly gained and which leads to a mutually agreeable contract. Of course, if you have lied or have no intention of fulfilling a promise, that is another matter.

> **Concessions to be sought and granted should be planned and the four ALWAYS rules kept constantly in mind**

Brinkmanship

The best known example of brinkmanship was the Cuban missile crisis in 1962. Here the Russians and Americans confronted each other on the issue of the delivery of nuclear missiles to bases in Cuba. The Americans said that they would sink any missile carrying ships that crossed their blockade; the Russians said that their ships would defend their rights to sail the seas. Apparently, the world was facing nuclear war. Eventually, after some very tense days, no ships tried to enforce their rights and no attacks were made upon them.

Although political commentators have written reams on the issue, nobody really knows what would have happened had the issue been taken beyond the brink. That is the real art of brinkmanship.

In using or facing the technique in a commercial negotiation, you have to decide how much risk you are willing to carry. You also have to be sure of your ground and be willing to stand or fall upon it. The brinkman who backs down has lost credibility and strengthened the opponent's position. Thus, the brinkman buyer has to have a good alternative source, while the brinkman vendor must not be particularly concerned with whether or not the order is gained.

The whole objective is to convince your opponent that you have all the strength on your side. This will not work, of course, if it is clearly not true. Good brink negotiators, however, do seem to be able to convince their opponents that they have more advantages than they often do. It is a technique that goes hand in hand with brashness and aggression. There can have been few meek brinkmen.

> **Don't behave as if you have nothing to lose unless you haven't**

Shifting sands

When you come across the shifting sands approach, it may have been used deliberately or it may simply be that the person concerned cannot discuss any one issue for very long.

With shifting sands being used against you, no agreement is possible on any issue that is being negotiated. Each time you think that a conclusion may be near, the topic being discussed changes. You then pursue this next topic until your opponent decides that the time is right to move on.

A similar approach may be used quite openly and obviously when you are probing to see if there is a likely basis of agreement. If you can find one significant point to agree on, a negotiation often becomes easier as both parties believe that further talks are worthwhile.

In political negotiations, this is generally referred to as 'talks about talks' and may be handled by officials prior to involving politicians. In commercial negotiation, it is often undertaken in writing or by telephone. Neither of these applications is true shifting sands as both parties are probing rather than avoiding issues.

The true shifting sands technique involves the deliberate avoiding of issues once they seem to be near to being resolved. This becomes a problem when used by a competent commercial negotiator because it is an excellent means of probing and obtaining information while giving very little away. Questions can be asked and further information sought and some snippets of information be proferred. When most of the useful information has been obtained or you start to gain some ground yourself, the discussion moves to something else.

If you find yourself on the receiving end of this approach, you first have to ascertain whether your opponent is very shrewd or very indecisive. If it is the latter, you have to take charge, and probably can without too much difficulty. You then run the discussion by pursuing the points you select and every time the opponent deviates from the issue in question, you pull the debate back on course.

If, however, you are facing a deliberate and planned application of the shifting sands technique, your attempts to put things back on course will be largely unsuccessful. To counter this device, you have to record each item discussed much more carefully and make it obvious that you are. Nothing upsets the negotiator trying to put you into shifting sands more than to discover that you have a separate page in your notes for each issue and that you know just where you are.

'Oh, very well then. We'll come back again to the question of the hatstands. Let me see ... according to page 7 of my notes, we were considering why they kept falling over.'

Never try to counter shifting sands with more shifting sands – everything will become so confused that you are unlikely to be able to retain control. The best counters are care and the application of routine record keeping.

• SHIFTING SANDS AND THE LAW •

A short time ago, I was asked by a defendant to act as an expert witness in a claim for extras on a contract. The plaintiff had also appointed an expert and we were instructed by the judge to meet and reach agreement on a number of significant technical points so that they need not be argued subsequently in court.

I prepared a list of key issues and thought carefully about my position as well as about the view that the plaintiff might be taking. When we met, I found it quite impossible to pursue any of the points I thought important. The other expert wandered around a great range of points some of which I felt to be relevant and some irrelevant. My inclination was to think him foolish but my negotiation training came to my defence and we parted without really getting anywhere. I felt initially that I had failed as my objective had been to reach agreement on as many issues as possible.

However, looking back at what had been covered, it became obvious that I had faced a very competent application of the shifting sands technique from an opponent who had been sounding me out and testing my position. Fortunately, natural caution had prevented me giving any significant ground but, not having kept thorough enough notes or having expected the approach, I had not been able to control any of our first negotiation session.

> The only defence against shifting sands is rock like determination and clear thought

Fogging

This is the technique of hiding an important issue behind a fog of irrelevance. If the approach is successful, both you and your opponent cease to focus on the key issues and start instead to examine the fog. An excellent example occurred in the same legal action that is referred to above.

The plaintiffs in the case were arguing that their plans for executing the contract had been disrupted and that they had thereby incurred extra costs. They then produced and tabled planning information that they had produced after the contract and solely for the purpose of pressing their claim. Discussion was centering upon these plans rather than upon what had actually been intended at the time of the contract.

Fogging, when introduced gradually into a negotiation, can be a very powerful device for avoiding discussion on a topic. It can be very difficult to see it coming and fogging is at its best when designed to be of specific interest to one or other person in the opposition team.

'The area certainly is one of outstanding natural beauty and we must make sure the factory blends into the surroundings. By the way, won't the east fence tend to restrict access to the trout fishing? How can we get around that?'

or

'Right, this scheme to demolish the main offices and relocate the staff into the factory is going to create a lot of personnel problems. Bob, I want you to get hold of 50 paint colour cards and be ready to hand them round ...'

> The only solution to fogging is a clear mind that does not lose sight of the objective

Hard and soft

The hard/soft approach may be easy to spot as most police series on TV have shown the technique in use. There are usually two negotiators, one very tough and uncompromising and the other almost appealing to the opponent to provide some help so that the awful person can be bought off.

Although this can be spotted if performed without subtlety, it can be a powerful technique if used carefully by two or more people, avoiding the extremes which make it obvious. When a solo negotiator changes character between hard and soft, the technique can also be very worthwhile, but is more difficult to apply. It may be appropriate to switch from soft to hard when the opponent seems to be getting the upper hand, particularly if that occurs because you have allowed yourself to be caught off guard.

Another use of the hard/soft technique arises when you are almost at the point of agreement, but have left some loose ends dangling on your way through the negotiation. Another negotiator then arrives, announcing that his role is to finalize the contract now that agreement in principle has been reached.

When you attempt to sort out the precise wording and details of the agreement, you discover that the loose ends are more significant than you had thought and all seem to be going against you. Not only that, but your opponent is not willing to discuss any of them. You may even find that completely new conditions arise, slipping in almost unnoticed. Here the solution is to be equally uncompromising. Your opponents have not gone so far down the road only to throw things away on small details. Maybe they are trying to gain a few points at the end but, if you are equally as difficult, they will have to compromise and you can meet halfway. That is probably where you would have met anyway!

There is a possibility that the opponents have decided that they do not want the deal unless they can squeeze out something more at the end, having given you too much during the main negotiations. This simply puts you in the position of negotiating each final small point and trying to find a satisfactory solution. Thus, the hard man coming in at the end is treated in exactly the same way as the earlier negotiations. Do not allow the sudden application of the technique to make you forget your *needs*, *wants* and *desires*.

Back burner

The back burner approach is used extensively both inside and outside the world of commercial negotiation. When you cannot reach a decision, you put the problem to one side and forget it temporarily. But just as in cookery, you have to remember that the back burner is alight and, if you do not sort out the problem reasonably soon, there will be an unpleasant smell of burning.

If you allow a point to be back burnered by your opponent during discussions, and do not subsequently ensure that it is brought forward and examined, it could well be you that is burned.

Sometimes, the back burner approach may be quite acceptable to both parties. It is most appropriate when:

- An awkward topic impinges upon an otherwise smooth flowing negotiation.
- Either side does not have the information needed to proceed.
- One of the negotiators does not have the appropriate authority.
- Other topics need to be cleared before a specific issue can be discussed constructively.

Let us consider each of these briefly and see how they might be used with success.

Perhaps you have had quality problems when dealing with a particular vendor but understand that these have been solved. The vendor tries to reassure you on the issue but you believe that some rather tough guarantees are needed. So as not to disrupt the flow of debate, you back burner the question, which might otherwise change the tone of the negotiation to your disadvantage.

'Yes, that was a problem and we must discuss how it can be addressed with guarantees in our terms of contract. But I think there are some more relevant points to clear first . . .'

Another possibility is that you may be asked for information that you do not have and where not knowing could make you less credible or spoil the route to agreement. It is not important whether the information is available or not, only that you do not have it at your fingertips.

'Of course we have the staff available. But in order to book them, I need to know more specifically what you require. I will draft out a short service brief and if it reflects what you want, I can let you know when we could start.'

There are many problems that face the negotiator who has gone into battle armed with inadequate authority. The first rule is to make sure from the outset that the right person is negotiating, but the problem can still arise. You do not *necessarily* lose face or lose the initiative by admitting that something is outside the scope of your authority, but there will be occasions when it could be difficult. At such times, apply the back burner technique by referring to another reason for your inability to reach agreement.

'Oh, discount in the form of travel vouchers. I would like to talk that over with the Social Club and ascertain what value they might place on them.'

The final point concerns the need to deal with certain topics before others. If the secondary topics arise first, they have to be very deliberately put on the back burner so that the prime items can be cleared first.

There will be instances when your opponent wishes to avoid a point and has in his own mind back burnered it. You then have to bring it forward again and ensure that it is dealt with first. In this case the opponent is attempting a diversion: you have to keep on the major road.

You might, for example, have a plan to gain a major concession and then follow up with a number of smaller gains. The opponent's approach could be to lead you directly into smaller points and try to leave little time for the more significant items. Whatever the reason, you should not hesitate to back burner the new topics until you are ready. Firmness can carry the day on such occasions.

'Yes, I can understand your concern about the hotels not being finished last year. But let me tell you of some of the new features that we have added this year ...'

or

'Yes, I realize that it can have electric door mirrors and an illuminated engine compartment. I want to talk about the free extras later. For the moment, let us concentrate upon the basic terms ...'

Just as there will be times when the back burner technique is useful in your hands, you should also be alert to times when it is used to your potential disadvantage. Whenever you spot it, do not necessarily react against it. Instead ask yourself:

- Why does my opponent not want to talk about that?

- Since I have spotted it, should I go along with it?

- Is this a perceived weakness I can exploit?

> Be firm in using the back burner when you wish to; take advantage of its use against you

There is one final point that is worth raising under this heading. When back burnering a topic, always try to refer to it along with a presumption of the conclusion. Then, when you raise it again, start from that presumption and work forward.

'Ok, that's the main points cleared. Now, about the free extras you were offering ...'

or

'As I recall, you were prepared to offer some pretty substantial guarantees against the hotels not being ready ...'

or

'We set aside this point about whose terms of contract we should use. Let's look again at any odd points in our standard terms that you might find difficult ...'

Russian front

Derived from the Napoleonic drive into Moscow in 1812 when the Russians simply fell back leaving nothing but snow and ice, the technique in negotiation is to allow your opponent to believe that you are on weak ground so that the whole of the argument against you is revealed rather too hastily.

There are two methods of doing this. First, you let the enemy think that you have retreated so fast he does not need to think of fighting. Second, you leave a few troops in view so that they can be seen retreating in a panic. Either way, the enemy rushes forward with little thought but for gaining even more ground.

The easiest application of the technique in terms of commercial negotiation arises when an over-zealous salesman has believed too much of his own sales literature. If he starts by being convinced that you really have no alternative, you may wish to disillusion him. Questioning about his company, product, quality, problems and so forth can be most illuminating and provide generous ammunition for the next stage of negotiation.

An alternative application is to ask in a gentle and persuasive way for more and more information, leaving your opponent feeling at each point that the deal is about to be struck, just one small step further will clinch things.

Neither of these versions of the technique is particularly difficult to use, but you cannot generally plan or prepare extensively for either. If the circumstances seem right, you may decide to adopt the approach without a great deal of notice. The penalties for being wrong may not be severe. If you start to retreat and then realize that it is not working in your favour, you need not have lost anything at all.

The third use of the Russian Front approach needs far greater skill and control. You give away a number of small concessions with little argument. *Some* argument is essential, but you allow yourself to be persuaded fairly easily. You may even allow yourself to appear weak and ineffectual. Your opponent should then be off guard and susceptible to granting a more significant concession, or may have become so deeply embroiled and committed that your subsequent requests – always put in the most apologetic of terms – are met with relative ease.

The Russian front need only be your downfall if you do not see it coming

As with all of these techniques, beware of it being used against you; particularly when the enemy retreats slowly, leading you on – that is the difficult one to spot.

Bomb blast

This is another technique that has a rather appropriate and descriptive title. The bomb blast requires you to produce something quite major and unexpected and drop it into the discussion. You then take advantage of the disconcerted opponent to gain concessions or information that might not otherwise have been achieved.

The secret of the method is timing. Something that may not be major at one stage can take on far greater significance at another point in a negotiation. For example, the carpet salesman does not tell you about the imminent price rise as you walk in the shop, but only after you have almost made your choice but are hovering on the brink of indecision.

The technique may also be used where a negotiation has been rather protracted and either side can say:

'This has gone on long enough. You know our views on the terms that would be reasonable. My managing director has told me that if you are not willing to meet those, we have to withdraw.'

Or the approach might be to throw in some quite unexpected information:

'If I don't buy these from your company, you will be off our supplier list and not in a position to do anything on the massive new project we will be announcing.'

Or a quite unexpected demand could be made – perhaps something that was earlier put on the back burner:

'I'm pleased we have been able to agree on that. It will be good for both our organizations ... I have one last problem; we had so many failures early on with the previous batch that I must have an extra 100 free up front just to be on the safe side ...'

The one thing you can be sure about when the bomb blast is used against you is that your opponent knows that you would not have accepted the extra demands had they been made earlier. So, do not accept them now. Remain outwardly relaxed (more body language), return to some of the agreed terms and re-open discussions. Find out if the bomb blast attempt was soundly based and decide how much credibility you must give it. Think carefully about your response as it will be the only chance you will have to eliminate the blast effect. Your opponent has dropped the bomb and cannot pick it up again – how can this be used to your advantage or be ignored? Here are some example bombs:

With the carpet salesman
'What a shame. But I am sure you could squeeze the order through a bit late. We cannot decide until at least Tuesday.'

When facing the managing director threat
'I will have a chat with your MD and see if he will move on some of these points you are sticking on.'

If the 'more business tomorrow' offer is floated
'What a shame. But if we cannot agree the right terms now, we would not wish to bid anyway.'

And, in the case of the free quality samples
'If we had not solved the problems to your satisfaction, we would not be talking business now. I'm very happy to provide an extra 100 on the same terms if your quality people need to be trained ...'

Correctly applied, the bomb blast can be highly effective. When you are the target, the most important thing is to take time to assess the significance of the blast and then find a way around it. Instant response is not the answer.

A well-planned bomb blast can be devastating, but make sure you understand the possible defences

---

Pre-emptive strike

When you know that you are likely to be attacked, questioned or criticized on a specific issue, an effective approach is the pre-emptive strike. You bring out an answer to the unasked question and thereby avoid being placed on the defensive or at a disadvantage later.

'Thank Heavens we've now completed that Russian contract. Being pushed into that really gave us problems. But with that done and our new Marketing Director on board ...'

The objective must always be to anticipate an attack and remove any possible substance from it. This may require you to approach the topic at a high enough level to imply that *all* points of detail have been swept up in your pre-emptive strike. The salesman in the example above has inferred that every difficulty with his service has been dealt with. He has also given unsolicited information – they had an unfortunate Russian contract – as a means of diverting the opponent to an irrelevant subject. This is an important feature of pre-empting – you must know what you want to be discussed *instead* of the subject you are raising and dismissing.

An alternative form of the pre-emptive strike is the *fait accompli*. Here you have not only anticipated the outcome of the negotiation, but have also taken action on that basis. You need to be sure that, if your opponent objects, you can hold the great majority of the ground you took – a small concession can be justified – as the technique looks rather empty if you back down substantially.

> 'We've thought a great deal about your concept. Our decision is that we will take 51 per cent of the equity, in line with our normal policy, for which we will put up £4m and the land. The contract is being drafted now for your signature. You carry out the construction and operate the facility for three years. We need to discuss the arrangements for operation ...'

There are some similarities to the technique of *biting*, the major difference being that the *fait accompli* is more generally used to jump towards a conclusion, while biting is a means of winning interim concessions. There are also elements of *brinkmanship* as you might have to call the deal off if your pre-empting is not acceptable.

> **The pre-emptive strike may operate in conjunction with a diversion and can eliminate difficult stages of negotiation**

Straw issues

A natural topic while considering the use of diversions is the straw issues approach. The key factor about straw issues, is that, once you get right up close to them, you see that they have no real substance at all. The approach needs to be carried through in a subtle way, as it is the threat from the issue which is more important than the issue itself. One popular use of the technique is to raise a point, discuss it in part only and then back burner it. There remains a threat that it will be raised and that you believe it to be significant.

Throughout the various stages of a negotiation, straw issues might arise but they must never be taken through to a logical conclusion. As soon as a conclusion is reached, both sides know how little substance there was and the issue has been of no value to its originator. If the topic can be discussed but *not* concluded, it can remain as a point of misunderstanding and possibly concern and may elicit a concession from the opponent.

There are two principal methods of handling straw issues when they are used against you. These are:

- Politely but firmly to continue to cover the issue raised until you can agree that it was not relevant in that particular case.

- To allow it to be back burnered but comment as it goes that you are pleased it will not disrupt the negotiation in hand: *if* it returns, either ignore it or talk it through in a relaxed way.

In fact, straw issues should be quite harmless. It is surprising that so many negotiators do not have the confidence or speed of intellect to see them for what they are and deal with them quickly and simply.

> **Careful use of straw issues can enhance your position; careful defence can destroy them**

Deadlines

'If I can phone your order through this afternoon, I can get it into our next production schedule – that will shave 9 weeks off the delivery time.'

'The papers go to our lawyers for the contract to be finalized at 4.00 pm today . If you can offer something better by then, your name could be on it.'

'We seem to have been talking about this for ever. I am worried about how serious you are. I am setting a deadline of 4.00 pm today ...'

The deadline might be essential or it might be imposed arbitrarily. In any event, it puts considerable pressure upon the opponent to complete negotiations. There is, however, a potential weakness in using the technique. If you are giving a genuine deadline, your opponent knows that *you* also have to agree by that time. The negotiator with the stronger case on any of the issues outstanding will thus be at an advantage.

Perhaps your opponent will allow your lawyers' deadline to pass, thereby giving you problems. Maybe the order will not be placed in time and there has to be an excuse that the production scheduling was delayed that particular week. Or perhaps you can simply carry on talking and making slow but worthwhile progress well after the arbitrary deadline.

So, if you choose to set deadlines, or if you quote deadlines that are imposed upon you from within your own organisation, ensure that your position is sufficiently strong to enable you to force your opponent to come to terms or give you the option of going elsewhere. If the remaining gap is too great, enforcing a deadline may lose you all the progress you have made up to that time. You may even be in the position of having to start again with another opponent but with no time at all available for negotiation.

As with so many techniques of negotiation, be very careful of imposing deadlines and then not working to them. Once you ignore or override your own deadline, your credibility suffers and with it much of your authority as a negotiator.

If you are faced with a deadline, try first to ascertain how positive it is and then ignore it. See if your opponent becomes irritated or edgy as time goes on. Decide to whom this deadline is causing the most difficulty. You may well be able to turn to advantage a weapon that was intended to give an edge to your opponent. If the deadline is real and to your disadvantage, you will have to decide whether to accept the outcome on the best basis and you can achieve or drop the whole thing.

> **Deadlines are powerful weapons but must be pointed carefully and not be allowed to backfire**

Dumbstruck

This is an approach to be used sparingly and one which generally cannot be planned. It is a powerful counter to an unreasonable demand from an opponent and can be more effective than objecting or asking for a break to consider the proposition. The dumbstruck approach is, in fact, most effective when your opponent is aware that the proposition is at least a little unreasonable. The shock of your response can then be effective in opening up the idea to challenge and negotiation.

A   What? I'm staggered, dumbstruck. You're not serious. Could you say that again?

B   Well, maybe you've misunderstood. I didn't mean to say we want *all* that. I only meant ...

If the opponent does not back away from the initial unreasonable demand, it may be because it was not seen as unreasonable or because it is intended that it be pursued as a firm position to see what ground can be won. If the first response does not generate some movement or indication of concession, you have to continue in the same vein. You cannot afford to move away from being dumbstruck – you have to demand a concession from the opponent's position or, if it becomes clear that none is to be granted, at least a powerful justification.

Perhaps B will stick with his position and react with surprise that you think it unreasonable:

B   Indeed I am serious. It seems to be a reasonable offer under the circumstances. We know our position and what we need to make this deal worthwhile.

A   I was right to be dumbstruck! Now I know you're not serious. How can you justify taking such an untenable position?

> **If you claim to be dumbstruck, you have to stay that way until given a good reason for moving**

Testing

In examining the many and varied techniques that are available to the negotiator, it has been seen that there are three different types of aim, namely:

- To obtain further information, of immediate use or to be applied at a later stage.
- To give yourself a real or perceived advantage over your opponent.
- To reach an immediate conclusion on a current point.

Testing quite certainly falls into the first of these categories – you do not expect to find an answer, or to gain significant immediate advantage, but to identify the flexibility which underlies your opponent's position. The information gained is generally soft – not factual but enabling you to make subjective assessments.

An example will illustrate what the technique is and how it can be applied to your benefit.

'It looks as though this matter of spares could be a problem. What would you think of looking at ways of dealing with the main supply and the spares separately? I'm not sure how that could be done but maybe it might help. I imagine you've had a bit of experience on that, haven't you?'

An unspecific open question is asked – or it might even be a vague statement – inviting the opponent to put a view indicating a way forward. The point that is made should be perceived as an attempt to be helpful rather than as a device for obtaining information. It should neither offer nor seek a concession but may hint that you have one up your sleeve if the response is favourable. Nothing specific should be proposed but ideas and options be floated.

An important factor in testing is that you must have reached a problem point that both parties recognize as difficult to solve. You then indicate a new way of looking at the issue so that your opponent is pressed into discussing the idea. In the statement above, there are a number of points of strength. These are:

- The speaker has the advantage of 'first strike'.

- There is recognition that a problem exists and that it could undermine the rest of the agreement.

- The question suggests a way of looking at the problem without inherently accepting a solution along those lines.

- The onus to find a solution is put on to the shoulders of the opponent: this is supported strongly by the inference of more experience on which to draw.

- The speaker is staying in control of the negotiation.

The precise words used by your opponent in responding may not be important. The most significant factor is the style of the response. For example:

The parry
'Well, we're willing to consider any approach that concludes this contract. Could you be more specific?'

The riposte
'Forget it. If you can't put forward a more sensible proposal, then I'm afraid we don't do business.'

The struggle
'Er ... well ... that's a bit difficult ... but ... I really don't know ... we are in a bit of a problem here, aren't we? ... I suppose we could do something like that ...'

The helpful
'That's an interesting thought. I don't think separate contracts would be worth the effort, but what about ...'

You may find that testing of this type actually achieves a satisfactory response immediately. That is not the primary objective of the technique as, if you were that close, another device would probably have been more appropriate. You do not generally use testing unless you have hit a significant hurdle and have not been able to overcome it by direct means. Generally, the response that you get will indicate what lines of attack are open to you and just how flexible your opponent is willing to be on that particular issue in order to reach agreement.

In fact, if your test produces a wholly unexpected and very satisfactory response, beware. Should it be that easy? Are you concentrating on the technique and missing the main play?

The important thing about testing is that it is one device among many. It can be used gently or more firmly and can then be pursued forcefully or you can back off, depending on your reading of the situation.

There are two stages in commercial negotiation when testing is most commonly applied:

- During early discussions when nobody is expecting specific conclusions and ideas can be floated and dropped.

- Towards the end, when testing can be a useful device for identifying means of overcoming blockages.

It is an interesting exercise to look back at the four typical answers that are given above and decide how you might proceed in each case.

> **Testing may be shallow or deep but rarely leads to immediate advantage**

Rounding off

In mathematical terms, rounding off means eliminating a number of extraneous and irrelevant digits. That is, you might round off your actual age of 33 years 11 months to 34 (or 33!) or, if applying for a new job, you might round off your current salary to the nearest convenient figure above. The use of rounding off is similar when applied to commercial negotiation when you might, for example, round off a calculated tender price of £19,247.76 to £19,250.00.

Whether you are a buyer or a seller, there will be occasions when rounding off a price can be marginally to your advantage. You assume that your opponent will feel that it would be seen as small minded to argue about a minor rounding off. There may well be a sound reason for simplifying a price as it may make subsequent dealings easier for both parties. Reference to a round number is easier, multiplication to allow for various quantities is quicker and VAT calculations can result in exact numbers.

But there may be wider implications. Is there any chance that the price you have rounded off might subsequently be multiplied by a large number, thereby making a significant difference to the overall price? Is there a possiblity that the agreed price will form the basis for other prices?

In other words, ensure that by rounding off for your own or mutual convenience, there is not a hidden implication that could become expensive. Of course, the converse also applies – if you identify an opportunity for rounding that would be to your advantage, then take it and see if your opponent objects.

Beware particularly of rounding off that appears for the first time when a deal is being confirmed. It may be accidental, it may not be particularly important but here again there could be a hidden advantage to your opponent.

When negotiating prices related to a number of like items you have to decide from the outset whether your best interests are served by discussing unit prices or the total price.

• PAINTED INTO A CORNER •

A buyer had been quoted unit prices by two suppliers of special paints of £1 and £1.14 per litre but it appeared that the more expensive paint was slightly superior. The rate of usage would not be significantly different but users expressed a strong preference for the more expensive paint. The value of the time saved would greatly exceed the difference in cost.

The salesman (who had done his background research and knew his product was preferred) pointed out that 14p was negligible for better quality.

The buyer was about to conclude the deal – reflecting the wishes of users and obtaining the overall benefits. However, just before placing the order, the buyer (an inexperienced negotiator, but a quick learner) worked out the total cost of the annual quantity of 35,000 litres in different grades.

He then reopened negotiations on the total price, obtaining the better quality at a nicely rounded price of £38,500, which he would never have reached had rounding off on single items been used. Of course, he also ensured that payment was to be made per litre.

In this case, an awkward litre price was justified by the overall cost saving that was made.

The final point on rounding off relates to a technique used quite commonly by auctioneers but also available to commercial negotiators. When an auctioneer is seeking bids a common practice is to jump in large steps initially and then progressively reduce them. Thus bidding might go in £200 steps up to £1,000 and then only in £100 units. If you wish to bid higher, you have to offer another £100. But what if, instead of nodding your bid, you actually call out an offer only £10 higher? Or only £5? You could well find that you have saved yourself £95.

Similarly, when negotiating prices, on whichever side you work, *you* should move in the largest units you can but counter your opponent's large leaps by insisting on working only with small steps. Do not allow rounding off to be used against you as it is by auctioneers.

There is a similarity here with biting and nibbling – rounding off would be the biting action, while nibbling is the way to counter it.

> **Rounding off can yield more money than may at first be obvious – always check the total as well as the unit cost**

Bad news/good news

'I've got some bad news and some good news. The bad news is that the pub has run out of beer. The good news is that they're giving away Scotch.'

or

'I've got some good news and some bad news. The good news is that we have been awarded an extra two weeks holiday. The bad news is that it's without pay.'

This technique, often used by comedians, has a serious side in commercial negotiation. It may be used when apparently offering someone an almost illicit opportunity or can be applied to divert an opponent towards a deal you prefer. We have, for example, already come across the carpet salesman who tells you of the impending price rise and then lets you know that he can sneak your order in by the back door at the old price – but only if you place it with him today. Much the same theme is adopted with the story that

'Our production schedule closes today but, if I can phone your order through by 4 o'clock, I can persuade them to keep a slot for you.'

The technique of closing a door and then opening it again can be used on a wide range of issues. It usually requires your negotiating opponent to take the next step, after you have revealed that it *could* be worth while doing so. As it is a device for forcing movement on your opponent's behalf and possibly obtaining a concession, your specific objective should not be stated. It is sufficient to indicate that the bad news can be countered only by a significant gesture from your opponent.

'We haven't placed that consulting contract yet but your price was some way above your competitors. We would prefer continuity with you but our directors are bound to go for one of the lower prices when they meet next Wednesday ...'

A powerful, but less obvious, use of the approach in the commercial field arises in deflecting your opponent towards your preferred deal. Here, you do not generally give the bad and good news at the same time. Instead, you leave the bad news to take hold for a while and then counter with the good news later.

'When you were leaving on Wednesday I mentioned that we will be throwing out your software as we are moving on to IBM hardware. As it happens, we might be able to carry on using it as long as ...'

If the technique is used against you, an appropriate counter is to ignore both the good and bad news and attempt to return to the position you were in before you heard either. Decide what was your objective *before* you heard the news; confirm in your own mind the *needs, wants* and *desires* that you had formulated. Then assess the impact of the bad news and whatever opening you have been given. You should certainly not assume that you have to shift your position or offer a concession. You should decide whether your opponents really have changed the battlefield as well as whether the news is equally as bad for them.

Taking the examples considered above, the questions which might be asked to counter the bad news/good news tactic are:

Carpets

- Is the salesman desperate to achieve a target?

- Is there really a price rise imminent?

- Is another shop offering a better deal? (and does this salesman know?)

Production

- Does the schedule really close today?

- What is the true impact if I miss this deadline?

- How much more will I find out if I allow the deadline to arrive?

Consulting

- Are they really likely to have lower bids? (and by how much?)

- Do they really prefer us and would they pay more for us?

- Do we want the business at a lower price?

Software

- Why have they bothered to open this door for us?

- Do we want to carry on supporting them?

- Does this say that they need us even more?

Many of the questions posed above can, of course, be asked in more than one of the examples. They serve to indicate that the bad news/good news approach may not have as much substance as it first appears and that it needs to be examined closely.

> **Bad news/good news can throw an opponent off guard, but not a thinking opponent**

You've got to do better than that

Here, the title is very descriptive and the technique is simply explained. When you feel that there is more to be gained from a negotiation but cannot see immediately how to obtain it, scorn the opponent's position as quite untenable:

> 'Oh, really, come on, I thought you were serious about this. You've got to do better than that.'

This can be most effective if carried through with an air of exasperation that you have wasted so much time talking to someone who really was not up to it. To be on the receiving end can be embarrassing, particularly if there are other negotiators on the opponent's side who inevitably assume that you are not worth doing business with.

There is one obvious response to such an attack:

> 'When you say 'better than that', which precise area did you mean and what exactly did you have in mind?'

but this will generally be countered with a sweeping comment along the lines that:

> 'If you don't know, let's stop wasting our time'

and you are no further forward than you were.

If you are to use the approach, be sure that you can carry it through. It needs a brash quality that should not be totally alien to the character you have portrayed up to then. It also requires that you are sure that your opponent does have some flexibility or concessions left. You cannot back away from the position without a very significant loss of face – and hence of negotiation credibility.

In view of that, when you are the victim of such an attack, you should not attempt to counter it there and then. Break off as best you can and return later, perhaps to summarize the agreement reached by that time item by item. Emphasize the points of agreement and then continue at the lowest level of detail until you feel that the attack – and any need to save face – are behind you.

You may even find that you can emphasize how constructive you have been and how it is the opponents who have been negative. Generally, however, it is better not to try to score points in this way. They may give you a great deal of satisfaction but do not contribute to the progress of the negotiation.

It is most difficult to counter this technique when it is used near a conclusion and someone more senior than your opponent arrives and asks for a résumé of the position. When it has been defined, he or she takes the 'better than that' approach and leaves. Under these circumstances, check carefully if your opponent is reacting and taking a different position and, if so, indicate that you are not willing to continue unless it is with the person who can make decisions.

> The 'you've got to do better' card can be powerful and disruptive, but you have to live with what you have done

Oh, by the way

This is not so much a negotiation technique as a finishing trick. Almost everything is agreed; all points have been reviewed; hands have been shaken; both parties feel that they have handled the negotiation well and reached a satisfactory deal. Then, as the door is open and you are about to pass through it, you turn ...

'Oh, by the way, I presume that it would be easier for you if we arranged the transport?'

'Er ... what ... well ... I thought ... er ... yes ... I suppose you had better ...'

The essential feature of this technique is that the extra item and its implied cost should not be too large in relation to the whole agreement and whatever you add on should represent something that is not second nature to your opponent and thus easily handled.

The approach requires you to conceal something and hope that it is overlooked and there are those who argue that this is dishonest. Others take the view that, if you were able to see it but your opponent could not, that is just part of the negotiating game. But honest or not, how should this practice be countered? The advice is very similar to that offered as countering many other techniques. You can either:

- Bring your opponent back, pick up the details and sort them out; you start at a disadvantage as you are immediately negotiating about an extra:

'You'd better come back. We need to look at that, don't we?'

or

- Think fast enough to dismiss the claim as already included in your agreement; that results in your opponent having to justify raising the issue separately:

'Absolutely. You don't think I would have agreed to those terms unless they included delivery, do you?'

Apart from the occasions when this tactic might be tried from an open doorway, it often occurs when deals are confirmed or when invoices are submitted. In confirming a deal, anything that has been omitted is simply added to the advantage of the person confirming. On invoices, whatever odd costs are deemed to have been omitted during negotiation are added to the main price.

> If you use 'Oh, by the way ...' be sure of your footing, be prepared to lose the point, but don't lose the main deal as a result

FOREIGN LANGUAGES

There can be substantial and often hidden problems when negotiating with people whose first language is not your own. Unlike many of the other difficulties faced in negotiation, it is generally *not* posssble to turn the hazards of foreign language negotiating to your own advantage.

Fluency

Beware of believing that you are fluent in a language or of relying on someone else who is and who negotiates on your behalf. You may well appear fluent when on a camping holiday in Europe but the requirement is much more stringent when negotiating, for example, the terms of a trade agreement with a foreign company.

If you really believe that you or your negotiator has achieved fluency in the appropriate language, you should also ensure that at least one deal using the same technical and legal terms has been negotiated before with your specialist in a leading or supporting role. Furthermore, if you cannot yourself test the person in the language, find someone who can *and* satisfy yourself quite separately that your planned approach to the negotiation is correct.

This may sound rather conservative, but the risks of not understanding the implications of what you agree can be high indeed. You should always bear in mind that understanding the language is one thing, but having a good grasp of how it might be interpreted by a court of law or an arbitrator is quite another.

It is generally better to have at least two fluent people in your team. It is also better to allow enough time for the negotiation to be taken step by step – at each step confirming the position that you reached last time. While confirming, use different words to define the scope of the agreement to ensure to the maximum extent that there has been mutual understanding.

Nevertheless, if your opponents are out to catch you, they probably will if you are working in their language without adequate care and advice. Your best defence is experience in the market, leading to an understanding of contract terms and, as a fallback position, knowledge of the law of their country.

In any event, ensure that you have reliable advice on the legal position on the contract you are negotiating.

Interpreters

Negotiating through interpreters carries all of the hazards of negotiating with a fluent but inexperienced team and quite a lot more. The opportunities for misunderstandings are substantial. You are in the hands of the interpreter for precise meanings and, with your lack of understanding of local language and culture, must inevitably miss most of the subtlety which might otherwise be discerned.

The best advice on negotiating through interpreters is don't, unless you are desperate for the business or can afford to lose on the deal.

Your interpreter might be a local agent who stands to profit from your deal. In this case try to avoid negotiating *through* that agent. Instead seek a satisfactory deal directly with your agent and leave the agent to do his deal with other locals. You may find that there is a need to negotiate part of the deal, allow the agent to go off to see what he can negotiate with others and then conclude your own deal.

If you must use an interpreter, it is a good rule that he or she should not stand to benefit from any aspect of the deal being struck.

Your own language

It may be obvious that, when negotiating in a foreign language, you have to ensure that you fully understand the precise form of the agreement and that your understanding is identical to that of your opponents.

Similarly, if your opponents are working in your language they may not have fully understood exactly the same as you. It is easy to fall into the trap of assuming that, because *you* know what you mean, so does the other party to the deal. Even when both negotiators speak the same language, there can be misunderstandings. When the mother tongues are different, this is even more likely.

It is not sufficient to say that any misunderstandings will be found when the deal is confirmed in writing. It is quite possible, for example, that a perceived significant difference in the confirmation will convince the other party that you are not honest. Thus, a simple misunderstanding might result in a loss of business and no further dealings with that contact. It is also worth remembering that, if there was a misunderstanding when you were face to face across the negotiating table, there could be the same problem with the written word.

There is little point in negotiating a deal with people who you know do not fully understand the terms. It is unlikely that the agreement will be fully executed and even less likely to be satisfactory from your own viewpoint.

Foreigners

A final word on this topic. Do not believe those who tell you that people of any one nationality all negotiate in the same way. You would not believe it of all the people from your own country, so why must it be true of foreigners? If, for example, you were told that all the business people in Manchester, New York or Paris had the same negotiating characteristics, you would not believe it. Why, then, believe that all Frenchmen, Russians or Japanese are the same?

• NEGOTIATING WITH ARABS •

I was staying in a hotel in Abu Dhabi and picked up my copy of a daily newspaper from home. It contained a feature about commercial negotiating, including the view that most British businessmen failed to conclude profitable contracts with Arabs because they did not know the two basic rules.

These were stated as:

- Never show the soles of your feet.

- Never be the first to introduce business into a conversation.

The following day, I arrived to continue negotiating with my prospective client and he produced the article. He was considerably amused and commented that, with advice like this, no wonder there were not more British goods in the local shops!

I shared his amusement, then introduced the subject of business and we did a deal. I had never intended to show him the soles of my feet anyway.

As my client pointed out, he moved in a competitive world. If he wasted all his time *not* talking business he would never do any.

Of course, there are some requirements which have to be borne in mind when dealing with people of different nationalities. The danger lies in believing that their negotiating approaches will always be the same. Blanket guidance on how to negotiate in a particular country is based on narrow experience (or none at all), is always misleading and can turn out to be extremely expensive.

LETTERS

Letters are not an easy means of negotiation and have severe limitations in many respects. But they can be powerful devices for preparing the ground for a face to face negotiation. In this respect, they are useful particularly for raising and clarifying the issues involved and for narrowing down the differences which have to be negotiated across the table.

One of the biggest problems with negotiation by letter is that, once you have put a view or a position down on paper your opponents are likely to return to it should you seek to change that position later. They can either insist on you reverting to the original position or can highlight the fact that you did not stick by what you said. As a result, many letters written during the early stages tend towards non-specific wording or generalization that skirts around the key issues.

A great deal of time can be wasted in exchanging letters that are attempting to obtain information about the opponent's position or are probing for concessions. There will come a point when little or no further progress can be made by letter and meetings are essential. Nevertheless, skill at negotiating in writing is almost as important as skill at face to face debate. The main difference is that you can discuss your draft letter with colleagues, choosing particularly those you know to be good negotiators and who are willing to challenge you on perceived weaknesses.

• LETTERS HAVE THEIR LIMITATIONS •

Some time ago I became involved in a post contract claim which was being negotiated between two parties. Everything seemed to have gone well on the contract until near the end.

Then the purchaser realized that the specification had not included a number of items that were essential and the vendor noticed that, although they would normally have been supplied, their careless omission from the specification had resulted in them not being allowed for in the costing.

Letters flew backwards and forwards containing accusations and counter accusations. After the initial clarification of the facts involved, nothing further of real value was put in writing which might enable the equipment to be completed and put into use. Nevertheless, letters were exchanged regularly, neither party wishing to be the one that failed to reply.

A large sum of money was withheld. Lawyers were being briefed and were ready to do battle. The Hundred Years War was about to begin again with heavy casualties on both sides.

Just before things went too far, it proved possible to bring the two sides together – well, almost. They started by negotiating through a go-between. Gradually the gap was closed with both camps admitting to some minor errors in the deal. They then agreed to meet and were able to agree on a solution at only the second session.

Some money was paid for the additional items, the supplier was invited to supply further equipment and each of the two managing directors respected his opponent's position.

What had looked like a disaster in writing was solved by face to face meetings.

Experienced negotiators know that most people are willing to be more flexible and reasonable when they are face to face with an opponent. Where there is a genuine will to achieve agreement and settle a deal, the face to face option is greatly superior to correspondence. Letters have their place, but less so when the issues become complicated, interwoven or almost finalized.

THE TELEPHONE

The telephone is a much used medium for negotiation and, handled in the right way, can be a means of obtaining more information than the letter and more even than the face to face encounter.

For example, on the telephone, buyers are more likely to give useful information as to why an order was lost than they are by letter or at a meeting. Somehow, they feel more relaxed, secure and apparently in control of circumstances while sitting in their own offices and will then be more forthcoming.

Advantage can be taken of this fact when preparing for a negotiation by telephoning various people in the target organization. By talking to a range of people, most of whom will have no involvement whatever in the subsequent negotiation, useful facts and background can be obtained. This is difficult to counter since many people will try to be helpful, believing that they are assisting their organization in its dealings with the person telephoning.

One major advantage to the person who initiates the call is that the time can be selected and appropriate preparation done. The recipient of the call was probably not aware that it would be made, may not realise the significance of the call or the questions and, in any event, will often be caught off guard. If the caller discusses another non-challenging issue of common interest first, and then moves gently on to the real reason for the call, the recipient can often be made relaxed and vulnerable.

If you are in control of the telephone conversation, you can also break off when you feel the time is right and call again when you have prepared for the next stage.

The art of telephone selling

A study of the techniques used by telephone sales people who call to sell 'personal financial services' or who are involved in religious canvassing can be quite informative as to good and bad techniques.

With some, attempts to say that you are not interested will be ignored with questions that you tend to answer, simply because they were asked. Gradually you are drawn in and can end up answering questions on personal issues that you would have reacted against strongly earlier in the conversation.

As long as the questioning is progressive and you are asked for more than yes/no answers, it can be quite persuasive.

It is surprising how many people who will state quite firmly that they simply put down the telephone on such occasions can in fact be drawn into conversation.

The same progressive approach can produce valuable information during the run up to a commercial negotiation. If you are on the receiving end of an unwanted phone call from an opponent before or during an important negotiation, be clear from the outset what you are prepared to divulge and allow yourself to go no further. It is not a bad rule to discuss nothing at all on an incoming call but, if there is a real issue to be covered and the telephone is the best medium, agree to call back, choosing your own time when you have prepared properly.

MAINTAINING PROGRESS

At one point at least in most negotiations, there will come a time when further progress is impeded by a significant failure to agree. This may be caused by a failure by one party to understand what is proposed, by a genuine difference of position, or by unwillingness to compromise.

There are many devices that can be used to overcome these blockages and maintain progress.

First, it is worth considering whether the reason for the hold up is real or imagined. Is there a misunderstanding? Is it deliberate? If it is possible to clear the hold up by explanation or clarification, then the negotiation can proceed. If not, then something else has to be tried. Many techniques were described earlier in this chapter for gaining ground and advantage during negotiations. One of those techniques, carefully applied, might get things moving.

Perhaps you have become bogged down by a personality problem. Are the people who are negotiating too involved personally? Have they come to dislike each other? Have they taken up positions on the battlements from which they will only shoot down upon the enemy? Of course, if you are one of the people involved, it may be difficult for you to admit that anything like that could be your fault. But is it?

To be a really good negotiator you have to be able to identify when you yourself have become part of the problem. If you have, either bring in someone alongside yourself or instead of yourself. If it is your opponent who is the problem, would that still be the case if *you* changed? Is there any way in which you can ensure that the opponent's organization makes a change?

Alternatively, if people themselves are not the problem, the negotiation may have become bogged down by a proposal that has been made but which cannot be resolved. If it is clear that further debate on the issue will not yield movement, retrace your steps, review carefully the troublesome proposal and, if you cannot see a resolution to it, try the approach that:

'I am not sure we can take that further at this point. Why don't I look at it and we can discuss it on another occasion? Meanwhile, I was very interested in what you were saying about ...'

This, of course, has been discussed under the 'back burner' heading and is just one of the ways of keeping things going. Whatever causes the blockage, and whatever means you seek for overcoming it, the important thing is to remember one of the golden rules of negotiating:

Wherever you are in a negotiation, always try to assess where you are likely to end up in your spectrum of *needs, wants* and *desires*

Having made this assessment, you may find it appropriate to sum up the points of agreement that have been reached with your opponent. It is easy when disagreeing to forget how much has been agreed and how much common ground has been identified.

So, go back over the points that have been covered. Use a relaxed style and highlight where both you and your opponent gave ground. Many stoppages can be cleared once the negotiation has been given renewed momentum in this way.

Perhaps by assessing your *needs*, *wants* and *desires* and by stressing the areas of agreement in this way you will see that you can afford to yield a little and still end up within an acceptable distance of your target.

Alternatively, such a review may demonstrate that you had not been thinking too clearly and should break off and take stock of your position. In any event, a break is a good way to overcome an impasse – it gives both parties time to think and may even persuade them to ignore the very point that produced all the difficulty.

If you believe that you can demonstrate to your opponent that the deal you are offering – the one that has hit the snag – is good, maybe you do not have to yield any ground at all. Go back over the reasons why your opponent should accept the deal; highlight all of the good things in it from his point of view; give him reasons why he should accept the deal. Many of the points you make could well be the very same ones that your own opponent will use in justifying the deal back at his own office.

Finally, if nothing you have done has provided the movement necessary to allow a deal to be struck, try stating the terms that you want. After all, if you don't tell your opponent what you were seeking, you may have thrown away the last chance of doing a deal. If your opponent does not like the target, you have lost nothing. If he thinks that it should be within reach, you are still negotiating.

A word of warning on this point. If you quote a target you have got to be willing to stick to it, or something extremely close to it. Otherwise your credibility has gone.

And one final caution. Just because there are so many ways of overcoming a blockage, do not assume that you *must* use one of them. You always have to be in a position to say:

'No, it has become clear that we do not want this deal on the terms that we seem able to achieve. I have an alternative. I am not locked in so heavily that I cannot get out. This negotiation is at an end.'

It is worth reiterating this point. It is very easy to become so embroiled in a complex negotiation that you forget that you have an alternative. The objective should not be solely to conclude that particular negotiation but to conclude a satisfactory deal either there or elsewhere.

8

The end is nigh

CLOSING THE DEAL

The deal now has to be closed. All the necessary work has been done and you are satisfied that a conclusion is about to be reached. You have, therefore:

- Prepared thoroughly.

- Devised your *needs, wants* and *desires*.

- Used the most appropriate initial strategy.

- Modified your approach as the negotiation has developed.

- Used the most suitable techniques at the right times.

- Countered everything the opponents threw at you.

- Seen through all the tricks that have been pulled.

- Given away fewer concessions than were available.

- Achieved enough of your objectives.

- Satisfied yourself that the deal is good.

Many good sales textbooks have sections about 'closing the deal', but the techniques are not only those of salespeople. Too often those who are on the buying side allow the vendor to take the initiative in handling the close. The good negotiator sees the closing of a deal as part of the problem and not as something which happens after the problem is solved. In other words, the negotiation is not yet over.

If we look at a number of the specific factors that can arise at this point in a negotiation, it will become clear that this stage can lead either to more advantage or to loss of some of what you gained earlier.

It is a good general rule that you should not deliberately avoid relevant but undiscussed issues to reach a close. The only possible exception is when you have a clear precedent on which to rely when confirming the deal. This applies whichever side of the negotiation you are on and almost however strong your case. It is also wise to ensure that your opponent understands the precedent.

There are four golden rules to keep in mind when nearing the end of a negotiation.

> *RULE 1*: IF YOU ARE NOT SURE, DON'T CLOSE.
>
> *RULE 2*: WHEN YOU ARE SURE, CLOSE.
>
> *RULE 3*: DON'T IGNORE IMPORTANT ISSUES SIMPLY TO REACH THE CLOSE.
>
> *RULE 4*: CLOSE EACH STAGE, BUT ONLY WHEN YOU ARE SURE YOU CANNOT USE IT TO FURTHER ADVANTAGE.

Some who give advice on closing a negotiation suggest that you leave as much as possible unclear, particularly where you might not have obtained the terms you wanted. While that may sound very attractive, the dangers outweigh the potential advantages.

Experience shows that everything left uncertain is the seed of an argument. If you are negotiating to ensure subsequent disputes, the best way is to ignore some essential terms and conditions deliberately.

Closing signals

A closing signal is any sign that indicates that agreement is close and that you are interested in tying up the loose ends and doing a deal.

There are two specific questions which have to be asked in respect of closing signals:

- Do you wish to disclose your view that agreement is very near by giving close signals to your opponent?

- Do you wish to acknowledge and respond to closing signals given by your opponent?

Closing signals can be easy to accept simply because of their implication that agreement must be near. Without adequate caution, there may be a temptation to jump from where you were to the final agreement, ignoring the route you would have preferred to follow. Be on guard for such tactics – they can be countered easily if they are spotted as all that is needed is to continue to discuss the issues you wished to raise.

Clearly, you can also use the 'instant close' technique if you wish to hurry your opponent over particular issues that you do not need to discuss further, or that you do not wish to discuss at all. Here, you deliberately avoid giving any closing signals at all – and ignore any that are put to you – and then quite abruptly bring the discussion to a close when you have satisfied yourself that an appropriate point has been reached.

Deadlines and pressure

In Chapter 7 the question of deadlines was discussed, together with ways of using them and preventing them being used effectively against you. Deadlines are an integral part of the closing stage.

In most negotiations, one side or the other is aware that there is a deadline to be met. Sometimes both sides are aware of the same deadline. Examples are:

- Ordering before a price rise.

- Booking production space.

- Agreeing a contract before a politician leaves a foreign country and has to announce the triumph.

- Settling a litigation on the court steps.

But there will be many occasions when only one of the negotiators will be aware of the deadline for closing and has to think seriously of any disadvantage which might be implicit in identifying it to the opponent. Here, some examples might be:

- Placing an order for materials essential for a specific run.

- Obtaining money to pay a debt falling due on a particular fixed date.

- Having to prepare a regular management report and needing the deal to improve the figures.

- Wishing to agree a deal in time to catch a specific train or plane.

If you should find yourself in the position of having a deadline imposed on you, for whatever reason, always keep in mind that a good opponent will probably spot that you are under pressure. You have to conceal this weakness in your position or you have to plan to overcome it. If you do not, you will be end-played as your opponent allows the negotiation to run towards the deadline and then takes the initiative to close at his own pace.

One final point to reiterate from our earlier section is that *during* negotiation you may by all means create an artificial deadline and state it to your opponent, but make sure before doing so that you are very firmly in the driving seat, whether you allow the opponent to realize that or not.

You can create serious problems for yourself if you use deadlines throughout a negotiation, allowing each one to be relaxed. Your credibility when you try the same technique at the close will then be lost.

Scrambled eggs

Quite a common practice if you do not feel that a negotiation has gone as well as you had wished is to confuse the outcome. In this way, you can either return to issues on which you did not do well or can hope that, in confirming the deal, you can state a position that was not fully agreed.

Scrambling the outcome in this way is not, of course, an honest way to do business. If you feel that the technique is being used to confuse the closing stages of a deal, you must ask yourself two questions:

- Am I dealing with a naturally confused person, or is this a deliberate application of a technique?

- To what extent is the confusion against my interests: which scrambled topics *must* I clarify?

In any event, beware of the approach, particularly when it is deliberate. If this was planned by your opponent, you may well be dealing with someone who cannot be trusted and where previous points – those that you thought were agreed – need to be checked carefully as well as those yet to be agreed. In that event, first decide whether you still trust the opponent enough to do business with him. If so, rely upon the notes you have kept, go back, clarify and try to discover what your opponent is hiding. Each point must be pursued until you are sure.

Never worry that your opponent thinks you stubborn and pedestrian; that is decidedly better than you and your colleagues *knowing* you are stupid and have been conned!

Summing up

Here, there are another three golden rules that cover this question very well.

RULE 1: **YOU** DO THE SUMMING UP.

RULE 2: USE THE NOTES YOU HAVE KEPT AND KEEP NOTES OF YOUR SUMMARY.

RULE 3: IF ANYTHING HAS BEEN MISSED, PRESUME THE OUTCOME IS IN YOUR FAVOUR.

One very successful sales negotiator with whom I worked claimed that he could gain more ground when summing up than in the whole of the previous negotiation.

To reiterate. . .

A number of points made earlier are highly relevant to the closing stage and it is worth reiterating them briefly here.

- Remember that you have to justify the deal you have struck.

- Similarly, give your opponents reasons to use in justifying their end of the deal.

- Rounding off at this stage often goes unchallenged.

- Beware of the line, 'Don't let's waste all this effort ...'

- Beware also the hostage play – 'Oh, by the way ...'

- Giving away your target *may* help close the deal where everything else has failed.

- Keep control right through the summing up and close.

You always lose

While closing, always give the impression that you have given away far more than you intended, have gained far less than you had hoped, and have only just managed to squeeze the deal into an acceptable range of terms.

Why? You may have forgotten something. There may be issues which are challenged subsequently. You may want to add something extra in to the deal. Your opponent may want to change something subsequently.

Even though you have closed the deal, many problems or issues can still arise. In other words, even after closing the deal, you are likely to continue negotiating.

'Qui desiderat pacem, praeparet bellum'
(Let him who desires peace, prepare for war)

Vegetius

CONFIRMING THE DEAL

We have now closed our deal and summed it up to the satisfaction of both parties. The participants shake hands and the negotiation meetings break up. But all is still not over. There is one final stage of the process to complete – confirming the agreement.

Many of the points to be borne in mind when confirming a deal have been referred to already in this book. However, it is worth mentioning them briefly again here.

First, always make sure that you are in the driving seat when it comes to confirmation. Do not allow the other party to send you the confirmation – you send it to them.

Second, always have the confirmation in writing and agreed by both parties. It is not adequate to sum up the agreement around the negotiating table and consider that as the end. You must then write confirming what has been agreed – this may take the form of a letter or a much more detailed contract document.

Beware of a response appearing to accept your confirmation but carrying standard terms and conditions on the back – it is a good general assumption that the last piece of correspondence on an issue is the one which carries most legal weight.

Just as you will have 'presumed' during your summing up – by stating your view on any terms and conditions that had not been discussed and finalized – so you may presume in the same way when writing to confirm. You may even feel that reverting to an original document, on which negotiation had been based but no conclusion reached, might gain you ground. There is nothing inherently dishonest about presuming in this way. The element of dishonesty arises only if you try to conceal or confuse what you have done.

The most important thing to keep in mind during this confirmation stage is the need for clarity. Always assume that the contract which you are confirming will become the subject of argument and legal wrangle. Do not allow that to stop you writing it, but do ensure that *you* at least believe that it sums up the agreement accurately and clearly. The acid test is:

> **Would an independent third party understand the same from this confirmation as I do?**

Ask someone whose views you respect to try to identify weaknesses and possibilities for confusion in your confirmation. If such things are there, you can be reasonably sure that they will come to light eventually, no matter how well you have negotiated the deal. It might even be the case that, the better you have negotiated, the more likely anything casual in the written document is to cause problems later.

You may feel that it would be appropriate to pass a draft of the confirmation of the agreement to your opponent so that all the features are clear and agreed prior to issuing the final document. Such an exchange would not normally undermine your attempt to gain extra ground as you should have chosen issues and decision points at levels just below the thresholds for major objections to be raised at such a late stage.

Never underestimate the ground that can be obtained during the confirmation exercise. Many negotiators will deliberately allow small things to be omitted from debate simply so that they can gain easier agreement during the confirmation.

REVIEWING THE DEAL

When all is over and the deal has been struck and confirmed, it is worth stepping back a little and reviewing just how well things went. Allow your mind to run through all the stages and evaluate how your efforts contributed to the outcome.

- Was your preparation sufficiently thorough? Indeed, was it too thorough?

- Did you have far more information and background than you ever needed?

- Are you really sure you did not misuse the information in any way?

- Could the preparation have been more cost-effective?

- Did your strategy turn out to be the most appropriate in the circumstances?

- Did you change your strategy? Was the timing or direction of the change right?

- What strategy was used against you? Was it effective? Why?

- Have you learned anything from your opponent's strategy that you can use in the future? Did you counter your opponent's strategy correctly?

- Were the techniques and timing you selected the right ones for the conditions? Did they all work? Which ones did not and why?

- What were the techniques used against you? Did any succeed? How would you deal with similar techniques next time?

But, overall, the principal question that has to be asked after any complex negotiation is:

> Did we come out of that as well as we could – If not, what have we learned for next time?

An excellent way of assessing performance, especially if you were negotiating on your own, is to discuss the events that occurred with a colleague with suitable experience. Simply by describing the events, problems and solutions you will find that the whole picture becomes clearer to you. In my own case, my most harsh but also most constructive critic is my wife!

If you have been negotiating in a team, it is important that the lessons to be learned are identified before the team breaks up or goes into its next negotiation. In team negotiations, there are some additional questions to be answered.

- Did you give the right tasks to the right people? Did you interfere with each other's efforts?

- Were you too many or too few? Should the team size have been different at different stages?

- How well did you interact and perform as a team?

Here again, it may be useful to invite along an independent person, both to provide additional wisdom and to draw conclusions from the debate.

'Lookers on many times see more than gamesters.'

Francis Bacon
Essays

9

In conclusion

All the preceding chapters have been oriented towards identifying how this purpose, set out at the very front of the book, might be achieved in different circumstances.

Many factors have been examined, alternative strategies evaluated, attitudes considered and tactics discussed. Throughout, however, there has been one underlying theme:

There is no 'correct' price for anything

Many aspects of negotiation are, of course, not about price at all and, in some cases, financial matters may not even arise. But the same concept is relevant to all aspects of the negotiation. There really is no 'correct' position at which to end. The end is reached when both parties have come to a point within their frame of reference where they can agree. Both have gained enough and neither has given too much away.

In other words, the opposing sides have probably:

- Achieved all of their *needs*.

- Obtained all of their *wants*.

- Gained some of their *desires*.

In stating this, it must be appreciated that throughout the negotiation the two parties may have been revising their positions constantly as they either manoeuvered themselves into positions of greater advantage or lost ground to their opponents.

As has been discussed, if the negotiation has been complex and protracted, the protagonists should each have been reviewing constantly their *needs*, *wants* and *desires* in the light of what they have been learning from their exchanges while, at the same time, developing their views as to the likely outcome of the discussions.

It is *not* a weakness to carry out such a review during negotiation. It is a weakness if such reviews result in giving ground because the other party has been cleverer or because the need for a conclusion and agreement has become desperate.

Similarly, a weakness exists if you have failed to achieve a satisfactory result falling within the scope of your strategy defined at the outset. The particular negotiation may form but one part of a greater strategy. The whole picture should not have been placed at hazard because the negotiation has not gone well and too many concessions have been granted with insufficient gain having been made in exchange.

Key themes

Two themes have run through all of the foregoing chapters and both are very important.

While you can draw on many different strategies and techniques during negotiations, you can be nobody but yourself. You can use traits that are part of your own character, enhancing or supressing them deliberately when and where you choose but, if you try to be someone quite different, you will fail as a negotiator. So:

> **Play on your own strengths**
>
> **Do not try to use characteristics which are not natural to you at least in some measure**

Flexibility is what gains the most ground in negotiation. Not necessarily flexibility exhibited in the form of concessions granted but flexibility in many other ways. You have to be flexible in selecting and implementing your strategy, choosing your preferred tactics, developing your argument, modifying the tactics used and evaluating the outcome. So:

> **Flexibility in thought and deed is one of the most valuable attributes of a negotiator**

Objectives

This is an appropriate stage at which to review the objectives which this book set out to achieve. The diligent reader will have found that the text satisfies:

Objective 1
To demonstrate that negotiation is not difficult.

Objective 2
To show that negotiation may be undertaken at many levels of sophistication.

Objective 3
To illustrate that all of us are negotiators already, even if we are not particularly good at it.

Objective 4
To highlight that negotiation can be fair, reasonable and ethical.

Objective 5
To put negotiation into perspective as a tool of strategic planning.

Objective 6 ·
To assist negotiators find the most appropriate approach in any circumstances.

Objective 7
To make us all into better commercial negotiators.

Objective 8
To prove that commercial negotiation, while being productive, can also be enjoyable.

But the most important thing to remember is that, once you cease to enjoy negotiating, once it ceases to be challenging, stimulating and exciting, that is the time to think of handing over to someone else.

It is, of course, possible that the mere thought of handing over will make you realise that you *do* still enjoy it – but don't hang on just because you cannot bear the thought of somebody being better than you. Step aside and use your experience to guide others – remembering always that they must be permitted and encouraged to develop their individual sytles and express their preferences for strategies and techniques.

Negotiating does require experience, it does require knowledge and it does require a good understanding of people, but it does not require too many years to become a competent negotiator. Time is not the main problem. The main problem is whether a potential negotiator has an adequately deep understanding of what the science and art are all about and the patience both to prepare thoroughly and pursue the subsequent exchanges with adequate diligence.

And that, in short, has been what this book was all about!

'This is not the end.
It is not even the beginning of the end.
But it is, perhaps, the end of the beginning.'

Sir Winston Churchill

Appendix

Using Negotiating Skills – Ticket Touts

During the Wimbledon Championships, there is always a lot of fuss about ticket touts.

Three types of view are expressed, which can be summed up as follows.

- *The organization people* believe that ticket prices should be fixed and touting made illegal.

- *The free marketeers* say that there is a supply and demand and prices should be determined by the market.

- *The hawks* suggest that the All England Club should set up its own last minute ticket auction system.

Let us assume that touting will continue and consider how you should negotiate with them. There are basically two ways.

The market study

Bear in mind that ticket touts do not make money unless they have strong nerves. Whatever route you choose will be tough going!

Arrive early. Approach all the touts and note what they are offering and at what prices. Formulate a plan – decide where you want to sit and the price you are willing to pay. Return to a few touts in turn and point out that they are out of line with the market. Select one tout and make an offer for the tickets you want. Indicate that this is a fraction below the other prices you have been offered. To pursue this line, you need five things on your side, namely:

- Confidence: you must demonstrate that you do know the market and that your target doesn't.

- Clarity: you must gather data, select your options and stick to them.

- Power: if the touts are working together and have agreed prices, you have almost no power in the market. This should quickly become apparent.

- Crowds: there need to be enough people about for the touts not be able to see each other.

- Options: you have to know that, unless you can negotiate the price you seek, you will find something else to do.

Brinkmanship

For this method, you have to be willing to forego seeing early matches and hold out until just before the big one. You then approach the remaining touts with about five minutes to spare and offer them 30 per cent under the nominal value of the tickets.

Trade offers until you reach a figure that is mutually acceptable or you decide that you are not prepared to pay the price that is being asked. Clearly, if you have time to include a market study, it will help.

Remember, though, that the circumstances are changing constantly as time progresses and a basis of negotiation established an hour before the big match is quite different for both of you from the basis five minutes before.

Advice for touts

But is there any advice for touts? Of course. First of all, try to establish a price cartel. Second, make sure that all touts appreciate that giving price reductions late in the day will only encourage more and more punters to leave things to the last minute. Third, never be seen to negotiate – nothing will cause greater concern amongst the punters than the feeling that it really is take it or leave it at your asking price.

A GAME TO PLAY

If you are running negotiating training, this type of role-play exercise can be extremely simple to set up and very productive.

Set out the Wimbledon type scenario to a few people defined as touts but don't give them a chance to collude. Give them target selling prices.

Provide separate role playing scenarios for prospective purchasers and, again, don't let them discuss their positions among themselves. For example, define:

- A Frenchman who has just flown over believing that he could buy a ticket at the door.

- A couple where the young man is trying to impress the girl with him.

- A tough businesswoman who very much wants to see the tennis but has her pride on the issue of cost.

- A businessman who had invited an important and prickly client but then found that he had been let down on tickets at the last minute.

It is not necessary to select personalities to go with the roles – indeed, it often works better if both buyers and sellers are cast out of character. But do allow enough time for people to get into their roles!

Index